Trust or Control

EXPOSING THE ROOT CAUSE
OF A WOMAN'S INABILITY TO TRUST

DORCAS STUTZMAN

For additional copies contact:
Dorcas Stutzman
PO Box 176 • Ronks, PA 17572
Email: straitpathsministry@gmail.com

ISBN: 978-0-9910171-0-2

Designed and printed by:

SCHLABACH PRINTERS

Sugarcreek, Ohio
schlabachprinters.com

My Dear Friend,

Many questions stream through my mind as I prepare to publish this book. Will I be able to clearly communicate the burden of my heart? What if people hate me for what I say? Am I really capable of doing this? So many questions, yet somehow so much peace in my heart!

We are all on a journey, and I am inviting you to travel with me as I share part of my own journey. The path may not always be smooth, but I beg you to hang in there with me to the end. You may feel unpleasant feelings stirring inside as you read. You may even get angry at me and throw this book across the room. I ask only one thing—hear me out to the end. Please believe that my heart's desire is for God's kingdom to come here on earth as it is in heaven! I weep and pray to that end.

I am writing this book primarily to women. There are many things that could be spoken to the men, but that is not my aim here. Do not let the enemy take your mind down that road and blind you to seeing your own needs! It is time for us to find healing so that we can think with the mind of Christ and walk in His plan instead of living and reacting through the filter of our wounds. Believe me, I know how deep some of those wounds can go. Been there, done that.

This book is not meant to be an easy read, but rather a call to repentance and healing. After all, don't those two come hand in hand? How easy it is to look out at others and think that if they would change, then things would get better. I call you, my friend, to stand up and LIVE! Put on the mind of Christ. Live as He lived. Walk as He walked. And yes, obey as He obeyed. No more excuses, no more casting blame. It's time for a total surrender to the cross of Christ, because in that cross you will find the very life and power of God.

I love you! Perhaps you are a friend whom I have not yet met, but I want you to know that I have already prayed for you. I long for you to walk in abundant life and healing. As the God of heaven allows the seed to fall, may your heart be the good soil that produces abundant fruit in His kingdom! If not on this earth, perhaps we can catch up on the streets of gold someday!

With all my heart,

Dorcas

FOREWORD

There are a few special, truly great people in this world. These are folks who have passed from the common to the uncommon, from the daily routine to what could be. These are they who have reached into the great beyond, touched eternity, and pulled eternal purpose into their lives. This eternal purpose illuminates them and enlivens them to be what others dream of. There are a few.

Among these few, some are women. They are women who perform the mundane, but who do so with such divine clarity that even the mundane breathes eternity. They may live in a mud hut, but were you to enter, you would believe yourself to be a celebrated guest in a palace. Only eternity will reveal how these few have shaped our world. There are a few.

Among these few women, there are an even rarer few who understand the time, the men they live with, and the children's hearts under their care. They have heard the Father's heart, and they breathe it into existence around them, into the men they love. They are not dissuaded by our mistakes and failures, for their hope is not in us as men, but in eternity itself, even as it is revealed in us.

Among these rare women are the truly exceptional ones with both a gift and a calling from God to communicate these realities to others in an anointed way. Add in the extraordinary experiences that shaped this author, and we are down to only a handful of individuals in the world. Let me just say for the record that I am ecstatic that she is my wife.

The book you are holding can greatly affect your life. There may be things in here that you do not like or understand at first. But from my perspective as her husband and the father of her children, allow me to say this: if she says it, sit up and pay attention. Dorcas knows what she is talking about in a way I find truly uncommon.

To Dorcas, my wife of twenty years, I say, "You still have it. The beauty and excitement of your youth has become a deep settled glow of glory that emanates from your spirit, washing over anyone who gets close. Thank you for allowing me to be close and for being the best friend I can imagine. You deserve to be heard."

To you, my friend, the reader: may God open your spirit to become all that He saw for you before ever you were born. May His Spirit rest upon you and lead you into freedom, rest and peace.

Stephen Stutzman

September 2013

Trust or Control

"THERE IS IN EVERY TRUE WOMAN'S HEART

a spark of heavenly fire,

which lies dormant

in the broad daylight of prosperity;

BUT WHICH KINDLES UP,

AND BEAMS AND BLAZES

in the dark hour of adversity."

Washington Irving

CHAPTER ONE
The Matriarchal Spirit – What is It?

Years ago in a distant land lived a young family. This family was probably very similar in many ways to my family or yours, just a husband and a wife and several children living together in a cozy house. One day a visitor came to see them and shared with them the beautiful plan of salvation. Although it was the first time they had ever heard this message, both the husband and the wife received it and invited Christ into their hearts and lives.

This couple lived in a time and place where followers of Jesus were persecuted relentlessly. It was not long until there was a loud knock at the door and soldiers arrested the young father, taking him to prison for his faith. In prison he faced the most awful conditions and torture one could ever imagine. The soldiers were determined to make him renounce his faith! Day after day he was tortured. Day after day he stood firm in his faith. The soldiers could not make him budge an inch!

Then one morning he awoke to the harsh sound of his cell door swinging open. Into the room marched the commanding officer and his men. They yanked him to his feet roughly as the officer sneeringly told him, "Today is the day you will renounce your faith! Today you will beg for mercy!" As the soldiers dragged him out of prison and took him away, the young father wondered. *What do they mean? Why is today any different?*

But when they marched him to the edge of a quarry and he looked down to see his wife and children in a little huddle at the bottom, they didn't have to tell him why today was different. He knew. They didn't even have to point out the pile of huge rocks sitting on the edge of that deep pit, nor the soldiers standing by to push them over the edge and crush his precious family below. He knew. In that moment, this strong, courageous young father, who had not wavered in all the previous torture, began to waver. Down at the bottom of that gravel pit were the ones dearest to his heart. Surely God would understand if he wanted to save his family!

Then, like sweet notes of music, up from the bottom of the pit came the beautiful words of his wife. Words that rang with truth and courage! Words that inspired a weary heart! Words that made a soldier in God's army straighten his shoulders and stand his ground to the very end. These are the words that she spoke, words that will ring throughout eternity! "Oh my husband, whatever you do, don't give up! Don't give in! Because tonight," she said, "oh tonight, my husband, we will eat supper with the KING!"

I still weep when I tell that story. It touches something deep inside me that is hard for me to explain, but I know it has to do with destiny. That is the image in which you and I, as women, were created! In a moment of crisis, pain, or even death, we somehow do have what it takes to seize a piece of heaven and bring LIFE into our little world.

I believe with all my heart that one of the deadliest enemies of that destiny of greatness is the matriarchal spirit. That spirit, sometimes referred to as a Jezebel spirit, is first of all a spirit of rebellion, which uses manipulation and control to gain power by whatever means possible. Our society has painted this spirit white and made it so common that it has become difficult for us to recognize. Nevertheless, it has caused great havoc in our homes and in our lives. I have seen it in my own life and in the lives of countless others. Let me share with you how it wormed its way into my life and how much damage it caused.

I was adopted into a wonderful Christian home when I was six weeks old. I grew up smothered with love from my four siblings and my parents. My earliest memories involve the love of my family and the small community that I grew up in, as well as the love I felt for my dad. We called him "Pop" and I was his little girl. It never seemed strange to me that even though it was my mom who spent hours reading me stories, my mom who stopped her work and played dolls with me, my mom who let me run off to play or help on the farm while she did my work, that it was my father whom I really loved.

Now don't get me wrong. Of course I loved my mom, and I knew that she loved me. But I was definitely Pop's girl, and I basked in the sunshine of his love and attention. His love filled many of the corners of my little girl heart, and I blossomed and grew. I had no way of knowing then what I know now. I did not cognitively know that my birth mother had wanted to keep me, but since her mother had a new boyfriend, both my mother and I were kicked to the curb, forcing her to give me up for adoption. All I knew was that in my little girl heart, I felt rejected by my own mother. Try as I might, I just couldn't feel my mom's love even though I knew it was there. I just couldn't get past that wall in my heart.

Maybe it was because I was raised in an adult household (I was eight years behind the rest) or maybe it's just how I am, but I grew up watching people. I still like to watch people. Our family traveled a lot because my dad was a preacher who enjoyed traveling.

I remember loving those trips, and loving to watch people... lots and lots of people. By the time I was a teenager I had realized several things. The first of those was that I never, EVER, wanted to be one of the controlling, accusing women that I saw. They could cut their husbands down to size with just a few sharply pointed words. I saw the resulting pain in their husbands' faces. No, I would never, EVER be that woman!

The second thing I was seeing at that time was an awful lot of strength and forcefulness coming from somewhere inside me. I was truly worried. What if I would one day become just like those women? Oh the horror! I vowed in my little girl heart to NEVER be like them.

Just to be safe, I devised a cunning plan. I decided that since I was a strong person, I simply would not get married unless I could find a man I couldn't push over. Pure genius, right? I settled back to see how it would all work out. In the community where I grew up, eighteen was the approved age to begin dating. I remember how with mingled horror and relief I realized at age eighteen that there was no one I knew whom I couldn't push over in one way or another. That is, until I met Steve! Incredibly, he not only didn't fall over, he actually pushed back! Needless to say, I was very intrigued.

To make a long story short, we were married several years later, and I settled in to be the very best wife in the whole world. I've always believed that if it is something you care about, then either do it 100 percent or forget about it. Anything else seems like such a waste! And so I set out to be the best wife that I could be. I was going to be the most kind, respectful, and submissive wife in the whole wide world.

In the first years it was pretty easy. It was just Steve and me and the babies. When he made a decision I didn't like, it was relatively easy to paste a smile on my face as I said, "Yes dear!" But oh, inside I would feel this churning turmoil, and my mind would race with ways to convince him to my way of thinking.

As our girls began to grow, their need for discipline became a huge problem and a point of conflict. Steve rightly saw that they needed to learn obedience and required occasional discipline, but all I could see was that I had to protect my girlies! I even remember that he once told me with his corny grin to, "Take a number and step in line!" for my own dose of discipline.

Luckily for me, Steve actually was an amazing father. After my instinctive panic died down, I really did trust him. He had proved himself over and over, and I knew he would lay down his life for us if necessary. When the girls were small they couldn't wait until he came home in the evenings. They even called for him when they needed a parent at night. It was wonderful! But even after all that, I would still have that ugly feeling boiling in the pit of my stomach whenever there was conflict. No matter how many times I did what was right on the outside, I could not get away from that "thing."

When the girls were still very small, God did an amazing work in my life. I had been rebelliously involved in some very dark things as a teenager, and that darkness had continued to haunt me until the day I fell to my knees in repentance. It is a long story, but suffice it to say, I was a brand new woman after experiencing God's deliverance! It was at this point that the Holy Spirit became an active part of my life.

God patiently gave us about four weeks to get back on our feet, and then He began bringing to our door people with some of the same bondages I had been delivered from. Since it was dark, occultic practices that had put me in bondage, it was people in similar situations whom God brought our way.

One by one, as best we could, learning as we went, we endeavored to help people get free from their baggage and connected to JESUS! Slowly but surely, we began to see a pattern evolve. We were seeing individuals, couples, and whole families with all the symptoms of having been involved in some kind of occultic practice or witchcraft, but we couldn't find the witchcraft. We spent time crying out to God for answers and reminding Him that we had not sought out the people who showed up at our door.

One week Steve and I were privileged to attend a seminar that focused on finding healing in our own lives. I will never forget the day when I was sitting there in a large crowd of people, listening to someone share a personal testimony. Suddenly God, by His Holy Spirit, began to reveal truth that would set me free! I remember writing and taking notes as fast as I could so I wouldn't forget anything. It was so real to me that it was several years before I realized that it was not the lady sharing her testimony who was sharing all this truth with me! My husband gently corrected me after hearing me share this story for the first time.

I was shocked to discover that the lady was speaking about something else entirely!

I remember when the download stopped and I was left staring at what I had written: three or four pages of my own willful self. It was so painful and overwhelming to see that in spite of how hard I had tried all that time to not be a controlling woman, I still was. I remember saying to God, "Now what? What do I DO with this?"

He gently replied, "Do with it what you would with any other sin. Take each thing, one at a time, to the foot of the cross and repent of it." I have no idea how long I sat there. I only know that I did as He asked. I would love to tell you that when I finished, bells began to chime, birds began to sing, and fireworks went off in the sky. Not so. I just had a deep, settled rest in knowing that I had been obedient.

We went home from that conference and had a few days before our family was scheduled to travel to a church where my husband would be speaking for a week of meetings. The very first morning back home, we were just finishing up family devotions when the phone rang. Seeing that it was Mom calling, I quickly answered it. I was very excited to find out that they were stopping in for a visit. That was a rare occurrence since they lived 2,000 miles from us on the West Coast. I remember planning with her that I would invite over some friends from our neighborhood whom my parents wanted to see while traveling through.

When I hung up the phone I became aware of a strained silence. Now for those of you who know my family, you understand that that in itself is a modern day miracle! Sitting across from me was my husband with a very guarded what's-she-gonna-do-next look on his face. On the other side of the room, my girls were poised for flight with a caught-in-the-headlights glaze in their eyes. I knew I was missing something, but what?

Steve finally came to my rescue by cautiously asking if my parents were coming, and then followed up with a very strange question. "Honey, how would you have responded to that phone call say...a whole week ago?" Again I was puzzled. What was he trying to say? And that was when the light dawned, and I began to see what God had done in my life earlier that week.

You see, control can come out of our life in so many different ways! One of the ways it came out in mine was in how clean my house had to be if my family came. I would bark orders like a drill sergeant! I had my girls well trained. They were poised for flight and ready to rush wherever I ordered. I was operating out of a need to control my little world.

That need went all the way back to when I was a little girl who could not understand why anyone would choose to stay inside and clean the house when they had a chance to drive a tractor. I well remember my family's expressions of pity for my future husband who would not like a sloppy wife who didn't keep the house clean. I know they were meant for my good, but for some reason those words went painfully deep, and when anyone from my family showed up to visit, I would be worn out from cleaning every corner before they arrived.

That day when Steve helped me to see that something had dramatically changed, I realized that life was never going to be the same. Something that had been a part of my life as long as I could remember was finally gone. That awful, dark feeling I would get in the pit of my stomach was gone! And with it gone, a whole new world opened up to me.

Let me pause in my story to explain to you as best I can how this control works in us. Maybe it would be easiest to understand if we look at what it is assigned to do in our lives.

It is better to dwell
IN THE CORNER OF THE ATTIC
then to share a house
with a disagreeing, quarrelsome
and scolding woman.

King Soloman

CHAPTER TWO
Assignments of the Enemy

A. Assigned specifically to destroy the manhood of leadership

This almost goes without saying. If something or someone wants to be in control, then leadership of almost any kind is a threat. This spirit is actually very anti-men. It will strike viciously at a man's vulnerable spots as a means of control. In extreme cases, nothing is off limits. I have seen this spirit publicly, boldly, and without shame exposing a leader and all of his faults. I have also helped to pick up the broken pieces of the affected hearts and marriages.

I have seen women publicly cutting their cringing husbands down in a circle of friends. I remember one lady who stood up in a gathering and asked for prayer so she could "hang on until my husband becomes the man of God I've always wanted."

Another woman would keep interrupting her husband as he spoke, keeping up a running commentary of the details he was either missing or that he had wrong. It was so painful to listen to! Later that evening the woman wondered aloud why her husband had shut down in a corner and wished he could be "more aggressive like your husband." My carnal self wanted to deck her, but I realized she had no clue what she was doing or what was driving her.

Many times, however, the matriarchal spirit manifests much

more subtly. Perhaps there is the look of disgust or the deep sigh that is meant to convey displeasure. Maybe we are simply quiet while someone else does our dirty work, or we mutter skeptical comments about our husbands' ability to lead or accomplish certain things. Whether we know it or not, all of this is designed to destroy manhood. Just because we have forced it underground does not mean that the spirit is not there.

Most of the time women who have controlling spirits are very nice to be around. As long as you walk the line and do things their way, you will be treated fairly well, but woe to you if you ever dare to confront them or cross their will!

I have watched as a woman manipulated and seduced until it was clearly not working, and then saw her turn into an angry, sarcastic, scornful, and arrogant shell who spit out shame and shredded any remaining ego in her husband. To add insult to injury, she later told me, "It was for his own good."

B. Assigned to manipulate and gain control by whatever means possible

Through the years I have often thought that surely I have seen all the "whatever means possible," only to have even more come along. This spirit loves to be seen but hates to be identified! It will preen and flatter you, but if you dare to call it what it is, it will quickly duck for cover. The matriarchal/Jezebel spirit uses seduction, womanly wiles, or sexual means to control men. If those don't work, it uses shame and sarcasm, scorn and arrogance. This spirit specifically targets the weak and the wounded, the hurt, rebellious and rejected. It uses flattery, smooth words, "prophecies" and tears to seduce these targets out from under authority.

Speaking of Jezebel, did you ever notice how she surrounded herself with eunuchs? Eunuchs have lost their inner strength and masculinity and therefore will protect Jezebel as their source of strength. They do whatever they need to keep her happy, because, after all, you don't want Jezzy upset! Instead of defending the man of God, they will rush to stand between him and Jezebel to keep her peace. Before you know it, the man of God has had his authority usurped, and he must now get approval and permission before doing anything or making decisions.

Ironically, Jezebel then turns around and berates the eunuch for not being a more aggressive man! I never cease to marvel at this phenomenon. I have had countless women complain to me about their complacent husbands who just "won't stand up and be a man like your husband is." Each time this happens I stifle my giggles and restrain myself from telling her how quickly my dear husband would infuriate her by standing up to her controlling spirit. When you castrate your man, you take away his strength and his ability to be an effective warrior for you or God.

C. Assigned to destroy the order God set up: God – Christ – man – woman

1. **To destroy femininity, thus making men and woman equal**
    a. **In vocation**
    b. **In role ("equality" in the home)**

2. **To destroy godly authority**
    a. **Finds it necessary to critically tear apart anything or anyone who stands in the way of its being in control**
    b. **May also flatter in an effort to control**

I am very alarmed by some of the attitudes coming out of the young girls I interact with. I hear comments like, "Whatever a guy can do, I can do better." Now maybe that seems harmless to you, but having been there myself, I recognize the snake behind it. What will a statement like that look like in ten or twenty years? And what effects will an attitude like that have on a marriage?

Satan is so subtle, and I really believe he has read the Bible because of the tactics he uses. For example, in our culture it is almost taboo to talk about headship order or women's submission to men. The first quote I always hear is, "In Christ there is neither male nor female." Praise God! I exult in that reality every single day when I enter into His presence! But ladies, somewhere, sometime, somehow we also have to reckon with the fact that the same God who in the Spirit made us neither male nor female, did create us by His own design to function best and be most fulfilled when aligned with His order of authority. Now before you begin throwing stones at me, take a deep breath and consider: if God Himself says something, why am I reacting against it? What is churning inside me, and where is it coming from? I assure you that is not a merely human response.

D. Assigned to destroy and block the soft, nurturing love of a mother in order to:

1. Wound the children

2. Destroy the marriage

This is a huge problem in our world today. I was once speaking about the matriarchal spirit at a ladies' retreat when a woman in the audience interrupted me and began refuting what I had been saying. I was a little taken aback, but since we live in a free country, she had the right to speak, so I simply prayed for direction. I felt very clearly I was not to challenge her, so when she finished I thanked her and continued on. In a very short time she interrupted again, and this time I saw a very clear picture in my spirit of this lady with a bucket of whitewash trying desperately to paint white what I had just exposed as black.

She ended by asking me how she would know if she had a controlling spirit. My flesh wanted to say, "My dear lady, you have NO idea!" But what I did explain to her was this: one way you can tell if this spirit is at work in your life is by finding out if your children can feel your love. This spirit is assigned to stand between you and your children and block the love you give them. It does not mean that you do not love them; it just means that they can't feel your love. I even explained how when you ask your child you will need to push past the initial response of, "Yes, I know you love me," and ask them if they can feel it. Ironically, this lady believed her children were now the ones trying to control her, and even when she found out her love was not getting through, she refused to look at it personally.

My husband and I have sat in counseling rooms with countless people. Over and over I have seen the devastation this matriarchal spirit has caused. I see it very uniquely targeting males in the home. While both girls and boys are impacted greatly by not feeling love and nurture, there is a very specific need in a little boy to feel that soft, gentle mother's love. I recently read the results of a study that found the same results we are seeing over and over in working with people. When a little boy does not grow up feeling his mother's love, he is highly predisposed to form addictions such as pornography or other forms of immorality.

The matriarchal spirit is one that brings intense pain. Resistance and rebellion always bring pain into our life. I have watched over the last few years as this spirit of rebellion has brought almost incomprehensible pain into young people's lives, even to the point where they become irrational. Ironically, they blame everyone EXCEPT the enemy for their pain. I have watched as perfectly sweet people get backed into a corner by this spirit. When they finally compromise in defeat, they do get a feeling of relief.

It doesn't take a rocket scientist to see where this is going. Suddenly, they are in a position where if they disobey God and agree with the enemy they get a feeling of "peace." And when they take a stand to agree with God against the enemy, they feel pain, turmoil and unrest. If an authority figure in their life even gently corrects them, the slippery snake of control viciously strikes out, causing them pain. Yes, you guessed it; they blame the other person instead of the snake.

E. Assigned to darken our minds so we cannot see our true condition or the lies we have believed

Isn't this spirit so easy to spot in others? But how easy is it to see in ourselves? Jill[1] came to me complaining loudly about her abusive husband who was so angry with her. It sounded awful, and I felt sorry for her! Then I began to find out the rest of the story. Her husband was angry because she and her daughters had just done something he had specifically asked them not to. When, understandably, he became upset, Jill could not seem to understand why. I am not here to defend unrighteous anger in any way, shape or form, but at that point what are the husband's options? Should he roll over and play dead for the matriarchal spirit when every bit of manliness in him knows it is under attack?

I've seen this spirit blind ladies to the point of insanity. Mandy was very upset because she believed her husband was spending too much time with their children's tutor. This tutor had to be hired because Mandy had left her family while having multiple affairs. The resulting trauma in her children had understandably caused them to fall behind academically. Even though she admitted she had no evidence, Mandy fired the tutor because, "She is too nice to my husband." Easy for us to see, isn't it? But Mandy doesn't see it. The last time I saw her she railed at me for not agreeing that she is the only who is right in this situation. And so the pain continues.

F. Assigned to bring spiritual death to our children by turning them from God

Many times the bitter acid of the matriarchal spirit causes children to reject what their mother believes. It also leaves a gaping

---

1 Except for the author's family members, all names and some minor details have been changed to protect privacy.

hole of resistance and rebellion in the atmosphere of protection in the child's daily life. I agree with an author who wrote, "In this nation, the Jezebel factor is the spiritual driving force behind the high divorce rate, the feminist movement, sexual permissiveness, abortion on demand, and the prominent place of women in the New Age and the occult. To see where we are as a nation, simply read Isaiah, Jeremiah, and Amos. One of the last letters to the churches strongly addressed the subject of tolerating the Jezebel Spirit. Revelation 2:20-23 gives a clear picture that Jezebel leads God's servants astray into wrong teachings or sexual immorality. Jesus in Revelation gives a strong warning of judgment on the Jezebel spirit. He also gives strong promises to the church which deals with Jezebel according to the discernment that God gives."[2]

We often sing a song about these being the days of Elijah. Will you stop for a moment and ponder with me? The spirit of Elijah, which was upon John the Baptist, was the forerunner to Jesus coming the first time.[3] Even so the spirit of Elijah in the end time will be preparing His church for Christ's second coming.[4] Guess who Elijah's enemy was? Yes, Jezebel sought to kill the prophets of God! I believe as the end nears and the Spirit of God is poured out on all flesh, you will see the head of the Jezebel serpent rising up to fight against God's anointed ones like never before! "Elijah" will be under attack once again because the spirit of Elijah stirs up and exposes Jezebel. So now that we know that none of us would ever want this spirit to have a foothold in our life, how do we identify it? How did it get there? And how do we deal with it?

Let's look a little more closely...

---

2 Sylvia Gunter, *Prayer Portions*

3 Luke 1:17

4 Malachi 4:5,6 and Matthew 17:10-12

Taking an alternative wrong trail

DOES NOT CORRECT

A PREVIOUS WRONG PATHWAY.

The only way to be on a

right road

is to get on one.

Stephen Stutzman

CHAPTER THREE
A Closer Look

The triangle is generally considered to be the strongest geometric shape. Its three sides brace and help to sustain each other. The matriarchal spirit is designed to operate in a similar fashion. It too has three main sides, and yes, they all cover for each other.

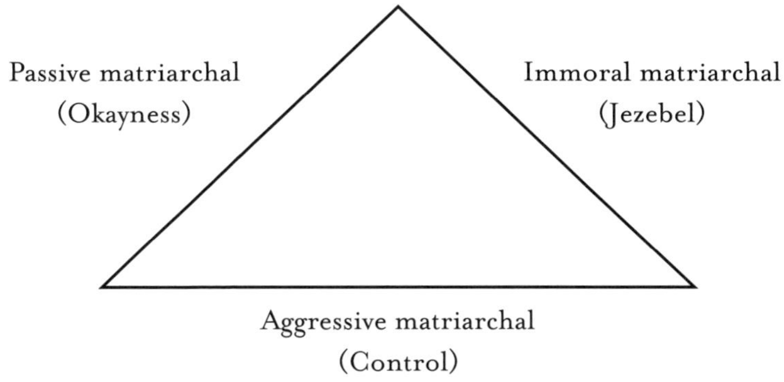

Aggressive Matriarchal:

- Openly controls and manipulates
- Uses stinging, bitter remarks and accusations to keep children and others in line
- Resists authority and believes she knows a better way

- Always right
- Hinders the sweet, gentle, nurturing side of a woman
- Inwardly resists the idea of submission
- Feels overwhelmed or upset if things do not go as planned

Passive Matriarchal:

- Covertly controls and manipulates
- Makes pain-driven inner vows in an effort to protect herself and control her environment
- Rooted in a refusal to deal with and accept life as God allows it to come, thus leading to rebellion
- Avoids conflict at all cost
- Driven to shield children from any and all pain
- Portrays false okay-ness with everything, even sin, to avoid conflict
- Makes image and appearance everything

Immoral Matriarchal:

- Uses favors and sexual immorality to gain control and manipulate
- Seductive
- Often dresses and uses her body to seduce and to get what she wants
- Uses her body to gain power

Here are some common characteristics of all three sides of this spirit.

Matriarchal spirit, whether aggressive, passive, or immoral:

- Controls through scorn, sarcasm, shame and fear
- Accuses others to get the attention off of herself

- Thinks the end she is pursuing justifies using whatever means necessary to get there
- 2 Kings 9:26 speaks of Jezebel taking Naboth's vineyard by wrongful means; this spirit is willing to rob a man of his inheritance of ministry or faithfulness, destroying him and his sons
- Is a very fearful spirit; through fear she rebels against trusting God
- Sets herself up as the final "right" authority and bolsters herself with records of past wrongs done by others
- Fosters darkened thought patterns that refuse to bow to the Lordship of Jesus Christ
- Urges her husband to compromise and do wrong[5]
- Very selfish, self-centered and Eros-driven. This spirit is the ultimate of flesh in control and life being about me
- Rooted in pride; it's always someone else's fault. Refuses to take personal responsibility

The bottom line is that Satan doesn't really care in which way we allow the matriarchal spirit to show itself in our life. He just wants us crippled and hindered from fulfilling God's plan for us.

Most of the time, we will find ourselves acting predominately out of one side of the triangle, but don't forget that all three sides are connected. While we may be more prone to one side or the other, we will often have crossover traits.

I have hesitated for years to use the term "Jezebel spirit." I have watched countless cases of spiritual abuse where leaders slung that term around indiscriminately. I want you to know that is not my heart at all. I have no desire at all to bring you down and humiliate you as a person, but I DO want to expose and bring to naught the slippery snake the enemy uses to defeat us and render us powerless. I am at war with that snake!

The Jezebel spirit is so, so much more than a seductively

---

5 1 Kings 21:25-26

dressed woman! As I stated in the beginning, the bottom line in defining this matriarchal spirit is control. But what IS control? What does it look like?

Of course there are those women we all know—the kind who will brazenly tell their husbands where to go and how fast to get there. Women who awkwardly interrupt and disagree while the man is talking, and who use biting, hurtful words to keep children and husbands in line. Women who are unashamed to openly challenge and resist church leaders and civil authorities. Women who must have things done a certain way—their way. There is even a television series that plays this up. Ever wonder what kind of marriage those "bridezillas" will have?

Now that the rest of us have given a collective shudder of horror, let's take a look at the passive side of the triangle. For those of us who grew up in church, we had at least some concept of how wicked it is to be THAT KIND of woman. But here is the bad news: many of us still had this same spirit operating in our lives. We were just a little more careful. And once it is there, no matter how hard we resist, it will eventually show its ugly head.

I could have been a poster child for the passive side of the matriarchal spirit. I carefully protected myself and kept myself in line by many inner vows and bitter-root judgments. Some of those vows were: "I will NEVER hurt my husband," (as I had seen others do), "I will not be controlling like she is!" or "No one will ever control me!" and the list could go on. Because of the deep inner pain that I carried, I built walls of inner vows to protect myself from more pain. I was so fearful that someday, somehow, I would slip up and get out of line. Fear ruled my life because I was trying to protect myself, since I didn't believe God could or would protect me.

During those years I carefully, oh so carefully, worked out my "submission" to my darling husband. If you asked him today if I was submissive to him back then, he would grin at you and say yes. He would grin because even though I was so carefully doing the right things, he often felt something that he could never put into words. He has since told me that he wondered sometimes when the "thing" he felt would turn on him.

I believe beyond a shadow of a doubt that God placed my husband Steve in my life as the one person who was not only patient and kind to me, but was also enough of a man to lead me out of this area of bondage in my life. I am so grateful that he loved me through it all!

I remember during those years summoning every bit of will power I had to suppress the desire in me to rise up and control. And you know what? I'm glad I did. I was not living in freedom, but I believe God has since showed me that my obedience (to the best of my understanding) was the catalyst He used to bring me to freedom. Nevertheless, I unknowingly began to shut down the passionate and courageous person God had actually created me to be. I believed that if I tamed and pacified my personality, somehow that would make me less controlling. I did want so much to please God!

While this stronghold was active in my life I was unable to be an effective helpmeet for my husband. To smother those awful, controlling feelings, I would just say, "Yes, Dear," to whatever he was asking me about. I had an unvoiced fear that if I ever actually tried to tell him what I really felt, I would lose control of myself and say and do awful things. And so I suffered in silence. I suffered not because my husband was cruel (he was not) but I suffered from the pain of bottled up emotions and feelings that I knew were not godly. I had no clue what to do with them other than to keep shoving them down in my box, trying to sit on the lid and forget them. I felt lonely and rejected. And the more lonely and rejected I felt, the more I felt the need to control by protecting myself from further hurt.

When God set me free from this stronghold it was a major re-education process for me! I began to see how Satan wants to rob us of true power in our life by offering us false power. My eyes were opened to accept that God made me aggressive, passionate, and courageous for a purpose! I began to learn to kindly speak truth as I saw it when my husband came asking for input. I also learned to simply give my concerns to the Father to carry for me.

I was amazed at the increase in productive energy I had when I quit wasting it on worrying and trying to control people. I learned how to take things to God in honesty. Things that hurt me and situations that were out of line could be taken to the feet of the Savior for Him to take care of instead of adding toxic waste to my box of life. And most of all, learning to choose to trust…to trust God and to be vulnerable to others. I was amazed how much Satan had robbed me! When I built walls around my heart to protect it from pain, I was unaware that I was also shutting out the deepest and most tangible joys of life. The joy of living opened up in a whole new way to me!

Today I am probably ten times more assertive and passionate than I was before God set me free from the matriarchal spirit of control. You may be shocked by that, but here is how it played out in my life: for years I resisted and silently rebelled against the way God made me because it stood in the way of my self-protection. I did not want any conflict or hurt, and the best way I knew to accomplish that was to be passive and quiet. Now let me hasten to say that passive and quiet were wrong for ME because God had not created me that way. Today I am free to boldly and aggressively speak His truth wherever I go. I am free to do this because there is no longer that icky compelling "thing" controlling me and pushing me. I can freely share my opinion with my husband and then let it go. I may not like the final decision he makes, but I can trust him and be at peace.

The bottom line is that Satan does not particularly care which ditch we are in; he just doesn't want us walking on the road. And Christ, our wonderful Savior, longs to walk hand in hand with us on that very road! No, He never promised easy, but He did promise we would be blessed if we choose that road.

How about it? Will you choose the seemingly easier and safer ditches, or will you choose your Savior? I promise you that you really can trust Him.

Making an agreement
WITH THE ENEMY
will eventually result in
*"pricks in your eyes
and thorns in your sides",*
regardless of how it feels
AT THE MOMENT.

Stephen Stutzman

CHAPTER FOUR
Open Doorways

So now that we can all see the awful destruction of the matriarchal spirit the question begs to be asked, "How does it gain access to us?" I want to look at several possibilities.

A. Generationally, or it runs in the family

Now before you begin to stone me for heresy, let me explain. Nowhere does the Bible speak about generational *sin*, but it does speak about generational *iniquity*. Iniquity has to do with inequity, an imbalance in your life. Think of it as the scales being tipped against you so that you're at a disadvantage while a particular sin seems to have the advantage. Iniquity is that extra push toward a particular sin. All of us know that if we were applying for health or auto insurance and we told them that our dad, our grandpa and our great-grandpa were all alcoholics, our premium would skyrocket! Whether or not we ever drank wouldn't matter. The insurance company simply goes by the figures, and the statistics say you would have that push toward alcoholism. The same is true of the matriarchal spirit.

Our youngest daughter was a newborn when God revealed this stronghold in my life. I never once thought about the possibility of her having an open door in her life. After all, she was just a sweet, innocent baby! However, by the time she was about eight months old I began to notice something that bothered me. Even though Karina loved her daddy, there was something I just could not seem to lay my finger on. Steve has always loved babies and is an amazing father. Our two older girls used to call him at night when they were little and needed something. It was wonderful! Now I don't expect our children to be carbon copies of each other (and are they ever NOT!) but there was a particular "touch-me-not" or "only-on-my-terms" attitude coming out of my little girl toward her daddy.

It was so pronounced and so real to me that I spent a week praying specifically about the problem and asking for wisdom to help me see the true nature of what was happening. God answered. I still remember it as if it happened yesterday. I was sitting in the living room having my quiet time with God when suddenly He began speaking to me. It seemed as real to me as audible words.

"Dorcas?"

"Um...yes, Lord?"

"Why would Karina NOT have a door open for a matriarchal spirit to influence her?"

Pause. "Um, Lord...maybe because she is just a baby?"I suggested a little sheepishly.

"Wrong answer, my child. Now go get her and deal with the problem."

I sat there in my chair stunned, even questioning my sanity. For a few minutes I wrestled with God. What did He mean, "deal with it?" How does one go about dealing with a spiritual issue in an eight-month-old child? As I wrestled, once again I heard the now familiar voice, "Just deal with it like you would in anyone else." Still feeling stunned and definitely way outside my comfort zone, I went to the next room and got Karina. Taking her back to my chair I sat her on my lap facing me and began speaking to her. I told her that as her mommy, I had opened a door in her life through my own sin. I further told her that I had repented and was going to pray over her, rebuking the enemy and asking God to shut the open door so that she would be protected. She smiled and cooed at me as I spoke, and I felt very foolish indeed. I decided right then and there that I would never tell anyone this story!

That evening when Steve came home from work a very interesting thing happened. Always before when he came home, Karina would sit among her toys and wait like a little royal princess for Steve to come and pay attention to her. That distant attitude was one of the things that had been bothering me, but this time when he came through the door something totally different happened. As soon as Karina saw him, for the first time she responded by throwing her toys aside and crawling as fast as her little arms and legs would carry her to her daddy. When she got to him she wrapped her little arms around his ankles.

Steve, being the dad he is, of course reached down and picked her up. When he did that a very significant thing took place. As he lifted her up, Karina leaned her head back and looked him right in the eye and then proceeded to tuck her little head under his chin and just snuggle quietly on his chest. Steve looked over the top of her head at me in astonishment and asked, "What have you done?"

Wow! Sometimes you wish it was a little less obvious, right? All I know is that from that day forward Karina was a very different little girl. Instead of the I-can-do-this-and-I-don't-need-you attitude, there was a gentle, soft vulnerability. I am still amazed at what God showed us that day!

Early on I used to believe that this spirit and its influence skipped every other generation. I would see a grandma who was controlling and biting with her tongue, and then I would meet her daughter who was as sweet as can be. You know, one of those ladies you just want to be around. The kind that is always concerned that you are okay, that you have enough to eat or drink, and that there is no conflict happening. About that time I would meet the granddaughter and, oh my! There was that control again!

The Lord had to open my eyes to see both the aggressive and

the passive side to this matriarchal spirit. Many times if a girl grows up in a home where the mother uses her words as weapons of control, then that daughter will choose the passive side of the triangle we looked at earlier. Out of the pain of the wounds she received she will self-protect and hold herself carefully in line so that she will not hurt others as she has been hurt. Then along comes her daughter (the granddaughter) and because she has never felt the sting of that spirit like her mother did while growing up, whoosh! Up comes the aggressive, the-world-revolves-around-me manifestation of control with no constraints.

B. Through deep wounds and abuse by authority

Often times when we are in a situation where we have been wounded and abused by authority figures in our lives, we walk away believing that we are defenseless and unprotected. The lie that we may believe is, "No one else will take care of me, and so I MUST protect myself." The devil does not play fair. We shouldn't expect him to. He will try to use a matriarchal spirit to motivate us (through fear) to protect ourselves through control.

Many times out of our woundedness we make inner vows to never be hurt again, and we take control of our own protection. God, being the gentleman He is, will step back and let us see whether we really can do a better job than He can. He allows us free choice. How often do we lose the gentle, nurturing care we so desperately want because we are determined to control our own safety? Because of our lack of trust in God, we essentially hire this matriarchal spirit to protect us. In so doing, we open wide the door of our heart for the enemy to shoot his arrows to hurt, wound, and incapacitate us. Which will you choose; trust or control?

Will you choose with the mind of Christ to forgive and release those who hurt you, or will you tuck each awful memory into that box you keep so you can pull it out if necessary? Will you choose to turn your other cheek to those who hurt you while you whisper, "Father, forgive them, for they know not what they do," and open yourself up to the pain, trusting God to use it for good in your life? Or will you build a wall around your heart so that no one can EVER hurt you while you silently accuse God of not doing a good job?

In black and white terms, if you have unresolved wounds in your life and you have embraced the lie that says, "No one else will protect me (not even God) so I must protect myself," and if you are living your life out of that lie, then you need to reckon with the fact that you have befriended the spirit of control. You have opened the door for the enemy to come in like a flood.

Today, many people in our churches, under the influence of this spirit of control, have become extremely weak and easily offended. All around me I see people taking up offense, even with God. "How dare He allow pain to come into my life?" they cry. When we choose control, we lose trust. We start to believe that if God allows my husband to get cancer then I am not obligated to trust Him any longer. Instead of believing and declaring that God is good regardless of our circumstances, we turn and walk away, determined to control our own destiny.

If we are living out of this motivation of control, then life quickly becomes all about me. After all, I must protect and keep myself safe. It's not long before everyone else must walk on eggshells around me lest I get hurt once again. If anyone has a different opinion than I do, they had better not bring it up! Some of us openly "blow up" while others do it ever so quietly, but either reaction is motivated by the same spirit of control. In both cases it has many of the same repercussions in our own lives and in our families.

Ironically, as we begin to micromanage our little world to keep ourselves safe, we do not end up feeling safe. We feel isolated, alone and very vulnerable. And the more we feel that way, the more we feel the need to control. Our husbands and our children take most of the shrapnel from our explosions, and the resulting wounds are real and painful.

Not long ago I read an article that was talking about the measurable effects that certain things have in our lives. One of those effects that caught my eye showed what happens to a child when a mother is overprotective and tries to shield her child from all the pain of normal life. I do not remember all the figures but I do remember the article stating that a lack of pain in a child's life actually stunts their emotional development and growth. I believe I am still reaping to some extent for doing that very thing to my children. I am so thankful for a merciful Father Who is healing us from the inside out!

C. Through Eve and through cultural exposure

In case you haven't noticed, our country and our world today are full of this matriarchal spirit of control. All around us are cries for women's rights and more power for women, including the right to have "control over their bodies" (which is actually code for the right to destroy human life being nurtured inside that body.)

In Ephesians 6 when the Bible talks about principalities and powers, it paints a picture of spiritual wickedness ruling in high places, or the heavenly, supernatural sphere. To believe that we can ignore this spiritual reality and not be affected by the principality of control all around us is naive at best. If we have not been actively fighting it, then it has most likely affected us far more than we realize.

All around us are billboards and advertisements and modern ideas calling to us to "Take what is yours!" to "Trust no one but yourself!" and "If it feels good, do it!" In some advertising the message is that women should use their bodies to get what they want. Girls are being actively taught in school to never depend on a man. It is all around us, so you are either fighting against it or going along with it.

Ever since Eve took her own way and ate the fruit in the garden, there has been a sinful desire to control born into everyone. It is very important to personally take responsibility for repeating the sin of Eve and to repent of any way in which you have allowed control to be a part of your life. As you do this, you may be surprised to find your eyes opened even more. The enemy loves to blind us to the agreements we have made with him!

Perhaps by now you realize that you personally have an open door in your life and have been either passively or aggressively controlling. Maybe you recognize how much control affected and wounded you while you were growing up. Quite possibly you see both, and you are wondering how to pick up the broken pieces in your own life as well as in the lives of those you have hurt.

For those of you who are in seemingly impossible situations, or have gone through them in the past, I want you to know I am not trying to minimize the pain and suffering you have been through. My heart weeps with you, and I long for your restoration and healing.

During many years of prison ministry, our family would sometimes do seminars and teaching in women's institutions. In spite of the crimes that put them there, my husband would often tell me that he met very few (if any) "bad" women. What we did find were many, many women who had been put in truly difficult positions. My heart always went out to them, and I often thought that had I been in their shoes, I would probably have made a worse mess by far than they did of their life. I have so much sympathy for them!

But ladies, at the end of the day, no matter what situation we find ourselves in, we will never make it right by siding with the enemy and his lies. He will try to convince us that we cannot trust our heavenly Father. He will try to make us believe WE are the only right ones, and will urge us to reach out like Eve and take the apple. He will try to convince us to turn away from God in order to isolate us, to intensify the pain and lock us down in despair. Two wrongs will never make a right in God's economy.

But do not despair. I promise you that there is hope! Christ is a Redeemer, and He does His redeeming work so beautifully if we will allow Him!

In case you're not yet convinced, let's take a moment and look at the fruit that comes from the tree of control. And if you're already persuaded, let me show you possible fruit you will want to repent of and cleanse from your life.

"A good tree
cannot bring forth evil fruit,
neither can a corrupt tree
BRING FORTH
GOOD FRUIT."

Jesus Christ

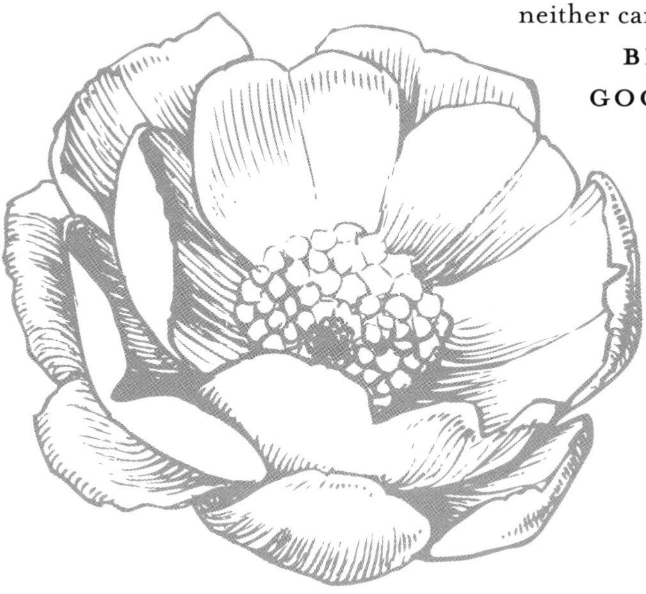

CHAPTER FIVE
The Fruit of Control

I am frequently asked how a person can recognize this spirit and how its tactics play out in our lives. To be quite honest, I do not have a neat or concise little answer. This spirit is an extremely slippery snake! Its middle name must be By-whatever-means-possible, as I mentioned in my definition in the beginning of this book. I have had it come at me with teeth and claws, and then when it was rebuked, it fell at my feet telling me how spiritual and discerning I was.

To be quite honest, I was more disgusted with the second, fawning display than with the first, combative one, although I do admit to wondering momentarily how badly I was going to get torn up in the first scenario! I tell you this story to make a point. This spirit will use whatever works to get its way. If being sweet doesn't work, then it will try pressure, or vice versa.

It is VERY important to remember that this spirit is simply using the person involved. The matriarchal spirit is not the person it is working through! Even though they must take full responsibility for sins and strongholds in their life, we need to remember that they are not the sin or stronghold. I know many women who truly love the Lord and desire to live for Him, but who are being badgered and manipulated by the matriarchal spirit just like I was. Be gracious as you would have others be gracious to you.

Having said all that, I do want to show you a number of possible ways this spirit may manifest itself in someone's life.

A. The matriarchal spirit HATES the word "No"

I have often told my husband, "If you want the matriarchal spirit to crawl out from under every rock, just say, 'No!' with authority." We joke about it, but sadly, it is all too true in many cases. I have had women tell me to my face that no man will ever tell them what to do or not to do.

In a conversation about this subject, Steve once asked a man how many husbands in his church would be able to kindly but firmly say no to something his wife wanted because he was confident it would destroy her. The man thought for a few moments and replied that he wasn't sure any of them would we willing to do that.

I was shocked! Has this generation of wives completely lost sight of the fact that our husbands are given to us as another layer of protection in our life? In our more honest moments, would we not admit that he is often better able than we are to make a judgment on any given issue without getting caught up by the drama and feelings of the moment? God hands us a beautiful gift on a silver platter, and we turn around and shred it to pieces? Please tell me it is not so with you!

B. It despises and distrusts authority

The spirit of control has a disdain for authority of any kind. It may manifest itself in your life by constantly questioning the motives of your spiritual authority. Its end goal is to spiritually emasculate and render powerless all spiritual authority by whatever means possible.

Gossip is a favorite tool this spirit uses to bring down leadership. It would love to have you yield your mouth to be used against spiritual authority. Be aware of the enemy's tactics and resist him in Jesus' name!

Sometimes the past wounds of our life leave us bitter and struggling to trust leaders. Satan will gladly use those painful memories to stab you continually and to push you around wherever he pleases. Wounds blind us so that we cannot see clearly where we are going. It is so very important for us to deal with those wounds by bringing them to the foot of the cross, repenting for our own sins of unforgiveness and bitterness.

Am I saying that your wounds are all your fault? Absolutely not! What I am saying is that you are still accountable before God for your response and for keeping your heart free from unforgiveness. As long as we are pointing our finger at everyone else who wrongs us, we will never be free. Our freedom will be found in honest humility and brokenness at the foot of the cross of our wonderful Savior!

Bitterness is a lethal poison. It takes a lot of energy to sustain bitterness, but more importantly, it separates us from God's forgiveness. As we say in the Lord's Prayer, "...forgive us our debts as we forgive our debtors..."[6] Every one of us needs the precious forgiveness of Christ extended to us daily. Nothing is worth blocking that flow! Find the grace to be generous and intentional in your forgiveness.

Unforgiveness is often based in fear. We are afraid no one will bring wrongs to justice. We are afraid we may get hurt again. And so we control instead of trusting, and our spiritual authorities take the darts we hurl in self-protection.

---

6 Matthew 6:12

C. It resists being under men in God's headship order as described in I Corinthians 11 and Ephesians 5:22,23

One of the ways you can know if the matriarchal spirit is at work in your life is by examining how you treat and respond to your husband. Ask yourself this question: "Is my husband free to make decisions?" Many men are afraid to make decisions because of the consequences they will face from their wife. If you are withholding favor, approval, or even sex from your husband in an effort to control him, it is sin! I have had women admit to me that they would give their husbands the silent treatment for days until they begged the wives to speak again. I have also seen men weep while describing how deeply that hurts and how trapped they feel by it.

The spirit of accusation works very closely with the matriarchal spirit. It often uses stinging, bitter remarks to cut people down and put them in their place. The words themselves, if analyzed, are not always that far out of line, but the sting behind them is what does the damage. The scars left on a husband's heart can last a lifetime. And the bitter acid of a mother's matriarchal spirit deeply imprints its wounds on the heart of a child.

This spirit also causes conflict in the home, which makes a man feel disrespected and unloved. Proverbs 14:1 says, "Every wise woman buildeth her house: but the foolish plucketh it down with her hands."

You can insist on being right, or you can be happy. Your choice really is that simple. Modern "rights" movements have convinced many of us that being right IS being happy. We've been taught to fight for that right-to-be-right. Look around you and honestly ask yourself how that philosophy is working out in our society. It is destroying marriages everywhere.

That "rightness" actually destroys our husbands' happiness as well as our own! I cringe inside when I hear a woman correcting her husband in public. If you ever find yourself doing that, STOP! Your being right is much less important than your husband's manly dignity.

Maybe you have also heard like I have from some women: "I just have to put my foot down, because he is wrong." I hate to break this to you, but he didn't marry you because of how right you were. "She is always right about everything, so I must marry her!" said no man ever. He married you because you were a fun, delightful creature to be around. He married you because he felt like a better person when you were with him. Then sometime after the wedding you decided you were right and always need to be right? What's up with that?

Think back to when you were dating and how hard you tried to please him and make him feel good about himself. Remember how much time you spent learning his likes and dislikes, his favorite foods, and what he liked you to wear? Would he have married you if you had treated him back then the way you treat him now?

I believe we often destroy the feelings of love and tenderness our husbands have toward us by yielding to the matriarchal spirit. Here's how it works practically: your husband comes home from work all excited because he ran into an old friend he hasn't seen for years. As he is heading for the shower he casually throws over his shoulder, "Hey, I invited him for dinner!"

Your dear husband is completely oblivious to the fact that the house is a wreck because you were working on a project all day. He has no idea that all you have for dinner is a pitiful little pot of leftover soup sitting on the back burner. Should he have called you on the way home and warned you? Yes, probably so, but he didn't think about it, so now what are you going to do? You have a choice. Will you think first of him? Or will you think of yourself and your image? Will you shame him in front of his friend and send them out the door, or will you serve that little pot of soup as graciously as if you were serving steak to a king? Your sweet graciousness in moments like these will bring honor to your husband and cause your husband's heart to be stirred with love for you, leaving you with the satisfaction that you took the high road. It's worth it. And it's the right thing to do.

D. It loves to hide behind religion and "spirituality"

The matriarchal spirit can put on SUCH a pious, spiritual front! It may say things like, "I can't give control to my husband; he might lead me astray." I'm sure none of us want to be led astray, but is it really that kind of issue? I would be the last person to ever tell you to disobey God (higher authority) but ladies, let's be real. Most times it is not a thus-saith-the-Lord issue, but rather a thus-saith-MY-opinion issue.

Another statement I hear a lot is this: "Since my husband is obviously not hearing from God, I just have to do this or that." Translated into plain English, that usually means, "He doesn't agree with me."

As I will acknowledge more in depth later, I do understand that there are cases of truly horrible abuse. My heart breaks for anyone trapped in a circumstance like that! My husband and I have spent many, many hours helping victims come to freedom and healing, but the rest of us dare not use those exceptions to get our own sinful flesh off the hook. Most of us do not experience what those ladies are going through, and we must not use it as an excuse.

The spiritual blindness that comes as a result of inviting this spirit to work in our lives is truly frightening. One lady spent several hours straight telling me story after story about her husband and all his faults and flaws. At the same time, she was upset that her children didn't respect her. When I finally asked her what she thought her husband wanted from her, she immediately blurted out, "Respect! But I tell him that is a luxury he can't afford." She quickly followed that outburst with the comment, "I just think God made my personality more spiritual than his, and if he and the kids would just recognize that, everything would be okay!"

I've met a woman who destroyed her husband's cherished family heirloom because she and her sister (see the generational bondage?) decided together that the Lord wanted it destroyed. Sarah called me to tell how angry and horrid her husband is. It sounded awful! I was beginning to feel sorry for her until I found out the rest of the story. Rather sheepishly she admitted that he was upset because she had deliberately defied him in two things he had good reason to request she not do. But she came back at the end with, "But he shouldn't get angry with me!" Perhaps true, but what are his options? Does he roll over and play dead while the matriarchal spirit castrates him?

On several occasions of praying through to freedom with women oppressed by this spirit, they have told me that as they repented, they felt like a sock or a stocking hat had been pulled off their face. Suddenly they could see more clearly with their spiritual eyes. What is amazing to me is the fact that all of them—without exception—immediately began to see and repent of their own sin before God. Isn't it interesting that Satan wants to first blind us to our own faults while bringing into focus our spouse's issues? But when we repent, God reverses that process. Where are you in that cycle, my friend?

E. It blocks the soft, gentle, nurturing side of a woman

The matriarchal spirit loves to go right to the core of our womanhood and strike at the very inheritance of our womb. One of the goals the enemy has is to destroy the close bond between mother and child so that the child will grow up feeling unloved and rejected even if the mother loves her child intensely.

I spoke with one 55-year-old man who told me he had never felt his mother's love. What is truly sad to me is that I know his mother and I know how much she loves her family and how little she understands how she has wounded them. I wish before God that this was an isolated case, but it is not.

Over and over men have struggled to share the depths of the pain they feel from this spirit of control. It leaves them feeling broken, beaten, worthless, and undeserving. They are left grasping at the tatters of their manhood, wondering if they really do have what it takes to be a man. I do wish that for one moment you could take in some of the scenes I have seen over and over in times of ministry. I wish you could see for yourself successful business men in suits, hardened construction workers, and tough, wanna-be gangsters all weeping and even wailing as they lay on the floor shaking from the agony of the wounds left by a matriarchal wife or mother. And then I hear women saying, "Oh, he's a man, he can take it." I just shake my head and want to weep too. It's real, ladies. It happens all the time.

F. It is selfish and proud

Whether it is the passive or the aggressive side of the matriarchal spirit that is being lived out in our life, there is a strong flavor of life being about me. If we aggressively try to control, isn't the underlying belief that I know best? "But," you may protest, "I am not aggressive in my control. How can that be selfish?" So you are quietly protecting *your*self, *your* surroundings, and *your* family. Hmmm...If you are using control to self-protect, where does that put God? Do you really believe you can do the job better than He can? That sounds like pride, doesn't it?

Along with that goes the attitude that I am never wrong, that it is always someone else's fault. A lady called me once to complain about the situation she was in. She had been involved in multiple affairs, had left her husband and children, and called me because she was upset. She was angry with her husband because she was positive she had seen him having dinner with another woman. No amount of evidence would satisfy her. Her own children told her that their dad was with them at the time of the alleged incident. She admitted to me that she had no hard evidence but firmly stated that she needed none. She just knew!

When I confronted her about the double standard of her accusing her husband of what she herself was actively doing, she primly replied, "It's not my fault, it's his!" Before the incident was over, her teenage son left home in disgust to "get away from that woman" even though she did not regularly live there. And so the cycle endlessly repeats itself. May I borrow your tissue?

G. It hates the prophet of God and his calling

A prophet points out sin and calls people to the cross. The matriarchal spirit HATES the cross. On the aggressive side, we avoid the cross because we do not want to be corrected. We would rather go our own way. On the passive side, our tendency to self-protection makes us recoil at the thought of suffering, so we do our best to avoid it. Our response, whether aggressive or passive, is still rooted in rebellion, fear, and a lack of trust.

We are afraid of pain. We are afraid of being exposed. We refuse to go there. The cross is pretty in the distance. Yes, distance is ever so much safer, but at a distance we miss so much. Our very redemption lies in that rough-hewn, bloody cross of Jesus! It is at that cross where our tears are mingled with His blood and we find new life and freedom. No wonder the enemy tries to keep us away either through rebellious control or fearful self-protection. You see, Satan doesn't really care which it is. They both serve the same purpose—to keep us away from true freedom and life.

My friend, you are at a crossroads. There are two paths before you, and you must choose one. The first path looks wide, safe, inviting. It is called control. The other path looks narrow, dangerous and steep, and it is shadowed in the cross. This path is called trust. One path leads to sure destruction, and the other leads to LIFE. Which will you choose?

Hurt people,

HURT PEOPLE...

Wounded people,

WOUND PEOPLE...

CHAPTER SIX
Wounding Others

It is sometimes difficult to see that this spirit is not only hurting us, but also using us to wound others close to us. If we had any idea how the deadly acid of the matriarchal spirit flows down over our husbands and children, burning and eating at them, we would fall to our knees in grief and repentance!

I want you to know that I am writing this book to bring awareness. I do not expose this to bring you to despair and unforgiving shame, but so that through understanding you will come to willing repentance and new freedom where Satan has tripped you up.

My heart breaks for any who are perishing for "lack of knowledge" as the Bible says. There have been times when I questioned God's call on my life. I didn't WANT to be a watchman on the wall! I didn't WANT to call people to repentance, because I feared what it would cost me. I have been brought to my knees repeatedly, and today I write for the redemptive plan of God in our lives. I long to see eternity and its perspective brought back into our homes and marriages. I pray for His kingdom to come and His will to be done in our lives here on earth as it is in heaven. I may never have met you, but I long for your freedom! I love you enough to speak about some tough things, and by God's grace I want to expose the lies of the enemy. And yes, I care enough about you to ignore the frantic lowing of your sacred cows, because I believe deep down you truly desire to align your life with God, His nature and His Word.

The way we allow this spirit of control to manifest in our lives will determine how it affects its victims. It is not hard to see how a controlling, my-way-or-the-highway spirit wounds and hurts. It makes sense to us that a wife and mother living out the promptings of the immoral side of control will deeply wound and bring insecurity to her husband and children. But what about the passive, oh-so-nice side of the matriarchal spirit? Surely it doesn't hurt anyone else, does it? Actually, it does. Let's take some time to look at the effects of this spirit.

Aggressive control is understandably painful to those caught in its headlights. It is self in control, defended by sharp, accusing words and bolstered by a belief in our own superiority. Its demeaning, cutting tendencies deeply wound the heart of a husband and block our love from reaching our children's hearts.

Control is especially wounding to our sons. This spirit thrusts deep the knife of inadequacy and performance; it attacks the very essence of a man. The gaping holes leave our sons especially open and vulnerable to anything that reminds them of the nurturing love their heart so craves and needs. Will Satan use that against them? Absolutely! We have found in years of helping people that almost every addiction we encounter comes from a root of not feeling loved. Every person is ultimately responsible for his own actions, regardless of circumstances, but I'm sure you want to give your son every available step up in life. You CAN make a difference!

As we will discuss later in this book, a controlling spirit cuts deeply into a man's identity and ego. Without that ego, he functions as a mere shell of who he really is. And yes, your sharp words wound him deeply and cripple his ability to open up and share with you the deep things of his heart.

Has your husband ever begged you in tears to stop criticizing him or to end the silent treatment you have subjected him to? That is his pain speaking! And believe me, the silent screams are perhaps the most gut wrenching. They speak of lost hope, of despairing of even being heard or cared about. It is easier to suffer in silence than to rage against the unmovable, unbendable spirit of control.

Control will shamelessly try to manipulate leaders in the church and will bring pain and suffering to those leaders with its actions. The vicious, accusing gossip and relentless nit picking have eventually robbed more than one man of his willingness to fight. The methods of this spirit of control are especially debilitating, underhanded, and strength-stealing.

When men fight, they trade a few blows and then shake hands, and the fight is over. Not so with us women! Our pecking order is defended by whatever is at our disposal. We tend to fight a much more behind-the-back kind of fight. This spirit fights in that same underhanded way. It uses cutting words and knife-in-the-back tactics that are hard to trace. It leaves a person bleeding, wounded, weary and confused. It strikes at the core of a person's confidence and leaves them second guessing themselves. And it desires to hurt others! How it loves to hurt in order to gain control! It has no qualms about putting its knife into any previous wounds or scars to get its point across and to establish control. When this is leveled at a pastor, husband, or leader of any kind, it is devastating.

As an interesting side note, I have observed that a son raised without a father and under a controlling mother will fight, not like a man, but like a woman. There will be minimal face-to-face or man-to-man confrontations. Instead he will be Mr. Nice Guy to your face, and then stab you in the back. In the old days of the Wild West such a man was considered a coward. It was a matter of contemptible shame to shoot an unsuspecting man in the back. I find it interesting how far we have moved from that concept of fairness. Could it be that the Jezebel spirit has indeed taken that much ground?

About twenty years ago my husband and I were privileged to be part of a series of revival meetings in another state. We prayed, the preachers preached, the Holy Spirit moved, and revival fires burst out. I can still see people lying on that cold cement floor, weeping on their faces before God. I was part of the team who prayed with the people who responded, and I remember that some of those prayers continued long into the night. It was a beautiful, holy thing that was happening!

Then slowly but surely the spirit of control began showing its ugly head through one woman. First it was, "Oh pastor, you really need to preach on ______." It was her pet doctrine, of course. When that didn't work, she began inviting herself into the private prayer sessions with people. Using twisted tidbits of the information she overheard there, she singlehandedly managed to destroy a fledgling church of new and rededicated believers. I watched in stunned horror as grown men cowered in front of that spirit. Looking back, I realize that she had done her homework. Before the conflict ever arose, she had everyone convinced that she was more spiritual than anyone else. The last time I saw them, she was leading the way, and her husband was meekly following with slumped shoulders.

Jezebel still surrounds herself with eunuchs. They are men who, for whatever reason, need to draw strength from her. In exchange, they will do Jezebel's dirty work. Perhaps they grew up with a controlling mother and never developed a strong identity as men. Maybe that is all they have ever known. I don't know about all the causes, but I do know that for a man to willingly be emasculated and robbed of the ability to reproduce is NOT normal. God even represents Himself as a strong, warring man in many scriptures. As hard as I may try, I simply cannot imagine Jesus with slumped shoulders meekly following His bride!

There is something both tangible and intangible in the strength and confidence of a man who knows his identity. The tangible may be evidenced in his brawny muscles or perhaps the ease and confidence with which he delivers a speech. It is the intangible this-is-who-I-am in his inner being that is perhaps the most valuable and precious. From this core comes the true essence that permeates every action, word, and attitude of a man.

As you can well imagine, there is a battle going on for the heart of a man from the moment of his conception. Can you grasp the possibilities for good from the life of just one man who has been properly nurtured and respected and praised by his mother, loved and trained for life by his father, respected and honored by his wife, and cared for and protected by a local church body?

Unfortunately, this scenario is far from common. We live in a fallen world, are born to imperfect parents, and often respond wrongly to the circumstances that come to us in life.

Satan very much desires to fatally stab and wound this inner core of a man while he is still a young boy. He desires to so wound and discourage the child that the man will never fully raise his head. He wants to debilitate a man's fighting skills and his courage—especially his courage. Without courage, which comes from a whole and healthy inner man, it is almost impossible to defeat the enemy. The insecurity and doubt caused by wounds are crippling to a man. They trip him up and choke him whenever possible, stealing the joy out of his life. This is what the enemy wants to do to your sons and your husband, and he wants to use you to accomplish these hideous ends.

If you think about it from the enemy's viewpoint, it actually makes perfect sense. Why lob arrows from afar when he has a chance to use someone inside the camp to do his shooting? Why not use someone who is close, who has knowledge of the weak points in the targeted victims? Why not use someone who may be swayed by finger-pointing and others' inconsistencies? Ladies, I think we have been targeted ever since it worked for him way back in the Garden of Eden.

Isn't it time to break the cycle? What if we as women could do our part without pointing fingers at the failures of others? What if we, by the grace of God, determined to bear the load and carry to the cross all of our own sin and iniquity? What if we stood firm in the face of the cause and effect of wrong choices made by past generations? What if we purposed in our hearts to forget what we think is fair and unfair, and what if we willingly suffered to change things for future generations? Can you comprehend what a difference you as just one person can make? What if all of us together picked up the mantle through a faith that sees the bigger picture, and instead of living in the here and now, walked into the realm of the heavenly and actually changed future generations in a positive way?

You see, the spirit of control locks us down in the here and now. It paints a fearful picture and narrows our vision to exclude the future. It is only in opening our heart to trust and faith that our spiritual eyes begin to refocus. What once was dim and blurry is now clearly in focus. And then, world, look out!

A mother's heart is a wonderful thing. It routinely does the apparently impossible. All of us have heard stories of a mother lifting a car off her child, or supernaturally carrying her ailing child over impassible obstacles, or even giving her life to save her child. She instinctively sees the bigger picture. She will endure all sorts of personal pain and loss to build a solid foundation that even she may not have had. She will not be sidetracked by real or perceived wrongs from others because she knows how devastating to a child are the wounds received in his or her own home. And when the enemy whispers, "But your husband isn't perfect," her sword and shield come up, and she stands against him as courage rises in her heart, courage that refuses to cower at her enemy's feet, courage that is faithful even unto death. Oh God, may it be so!

Many of you probably live with a man who has been repeatedly wounded by this spirit of control, so I don't have to tell you how painful it can be to experience the reaction from his wounds. I know. Sometimes you might just want to throw up your hands in despair because it just isn't fair. But then, who promised fairness? Life is never going to be absolutely fair. The question is, "What are we going to do with what we get?" Will we sit in the corner and sulk, refusing to move until we get what we want? Will we dish out to others what we feel we are receiving, hoping to balance our pain with theirs? Or will we allow that eternal courage to rise up into our hearts to access what God actually did promise—His grace?

Grace is God's ability to write His divinity on our hearts, to give us the courage and strength to meet what we are facing, and to express His divine nature in our human body. Did someone say that grace is AMAZING?!

Sadly, even amazing grace can be limited. It is never limited from God's end, but we have the capacity to limit grace from our end. Grace will never be fully and completely experienced if we refuse to open our hearts to trust. Grace often stands waiting outside our folded arms and protective walls. So many times God longs to wash over us with a flood of His grace, but we only get a few drops splashing over the walls of control and self protection we have built. As the parched soil of our heart cries out, the enemy smiles. He knows it is only a matter of time until we turn and blame God. So goes the cycle of control. Not much has changed since the Garden of Eden.

The choice comes back to each one of us. We can continue living in the shadow of past generations and our own sin, or we can turn our faces to a better way. It's a way that looks horrifying to our flesh and spiritually unfocused eyes. It's a way that involves death at the foot of the cross, a way that brings new life and resurrection power to the believing, trusting heart. Which will you choose; trust or control?

Love takes off masks

THAT WE FEAR WE CANNOT
LIVE WITHOUT,

and KNOW we cannot live within.

James A. Baldwin

CHAPTER SEVEN
Monster of Fear

Ungodly fear is a major component of the matriarchal spirit. With its forked tongue, it whispers its lying half-truths into our soul. It slithers through our conscious and unconscious memory, and with a slash of its fangs, brings to the surface old memories infected with the bitter venom it releases. With each reminder we cling a little more tightly to the tatters of self we are trying to protect. Each slash of the fangs reminds us of the pain we are protecting ourselves from, and the bitter venom proves to us once again that we can trust no one.

What is fear? Fear is defined as being afraid, worried, scared and anxious that something bad is about to happen. Ungodly fear is actually a spiritual problem, but it manifests itself in different ways.

- Fear is not trusting God
- Fear is a lack of faith
- Fear is an agreement with the enemy of our souls
- Fear is the opposite of trusting God and faith
- Fear comes from lack of identity and intimacy with the Father

It is not too hard to see how Satan can use fear in our lives to gain a foothold. 2 Timothy 1:7 says that God has "...not given us the spirit of fear; but of power, and of love, and of a sound mind."

Over and over I have seen people so controlled by fear that I start to worry for their sanity! Fear seems so rational, but only to the one who is being tormented by it. Fear can cause us to behave insanely. It is not our friend—it wants to destroy us! It wants us to believe its lies and allow them to wreck the relationships in our lives. I know a tall, slender lady who weighs less than a hundred pounds, yet she is unable to ever let her husband see her undressed because she is so afraid she is fat. Can you see that as a potential problem in a marriage? Another lady was so paralyzed by fear of her wedding night that it was months before they consummated their marriage and she found that what she feared was not true at all.

I believe ungodly fear is a strategic battle plan of the enemy. Think it through with me. The Bible says that without faith it is impossible to please God. So if the enemy can plant seeds of fear in our hearts, and if those seeds take root without our recognizing them and pulling them out, they will produce a lush crop of fear. That fear has roots of doubt and unbelief about God's ability to protect and care for us. Can you see where this is going?

We must learn to recognize the enemy. Often he will throw in just enough truth to make us fall for the lie and give in to fear. But he does NOT speak the truth!

He may say to you, "See that cliff over there? Your car may blow a tire and send you over the edge. You need to be very afraid!" And you know, that could actually happen, so we agree with him in fear, and then panic sets in.

The truth is this: even if all those things happen, I am in my Father's care. He loves me and will care for me. And if I should die, then I will see Him and be in His presence! Now that is TRUTH!

Fear is a paralyzing leash that holds you back from truly living.

It is a mountain, and you have the power to move it in Jesus' name.

1 Samuel 30 tells the story of how David and his men returned from battle to find their city burned and their wives and children taken captive. As if that wasn't bad enough, David's men turned on him in their disappointment and anger, actually threatening to kill him. Add to that the fact that his own family was missing and he was exhausted. It seems to me that the serpent of fear must have been all coiled up and ready to strike. Did David give in to fear? No! The Bible records that "David encouraged himself in the LORD his God."

So many times we find ourselves in tough situations, including some that are so terrible that even onlookers would understand if we gave in to fear. But fear is actually a chain that keeps us pinned to the earth and prevents us from reaching the realm of divinity. It roots us to the present circumstance to keep us from looking in the God-mirror, which reflects faith instead of fear.

For years Rachel lived in mostly silent fear. She was fearful every time her husband made a decision. If it had to do with finances, she was nearly paralyzed with panic. She fretted and worried. She tried to drop hints to her husband to control his decisions. Even when they prospered financially, she could not let down her guard.

You see, when Rachel was a teenager, her dad had made a bad business decision and lost everything. Way back then, fear had whispered to Rachel that she should never trust a man to provide for her. As Rachel listened and agreed with fear, trust slid out the door and control moved in.

For years Rachel suffered, until one day through the amazing grace of God, her eyes were opened as she heard a message about the matriarchal spirit. As God opened the eyes of her heart, she realized that years ago fear had opened the door to let in the controlling spirit she had lived with for most of her life. She sat weeping as she saw how Satan had robbed her all those years, robbed her of joy and rest and peace and relationships. Tears ran down her face as I prayed for that stronghold to be broken in her life and asked God to restore to her the years that the cankerworm had eaten.[7] I am thrilled to tell you that God has greatly restored her life! The peace and joy that radiate from her and her whole family is a testament to the redemption that Jesus offers. Praise Him!

You may wonder why the Bible says that we should fear the Lord[8] and that the fear of the Lord is the beginning of wisdom.[9] You may have noticed I began this chapter with the words "ungodly fear." I very much believe there is such a thing as godly fear. It has to do with respect, awe, and humility in the presence of a holy God. It has to do with understanding that although God loves us tenderly and compassionately and cares for our heart, there is also an element in the character of God that should make us fall to our knees in reverent fear.

I weep because of the devastation, pain and suffering that ungodly fear produces in homes and lives. I weep also because we have unknowingly portrayed in our marriages a very wrong image of Christ and the church. I want to once again see Jesus the Bridegroom, riding on His white horse in power, authority, and strength. I want to see His eyes flash with righteous fire and to see the glint of his sword. I want to see Him in full battle gear with His sword in one hand, stooping to pick up and rescue a wounded child with the other. I want to be a part of his bride-to-be who falls to her knees in respect and reverence as He approaches. I want to see the look of manly admiration and protective love in His eyes as He dismounts and takes her by the hand. I want to feel the mutual understanding of His steadfast, warring, protective love that has been fueled by honor, respect and deference from His bride-to-be. Oh God, may it be so, not for my sake but for Yours! May the glory of Your presence once again fall on our marriages and cause us to reveal Your goodness!

I hope by now I have painted an adequate picture of how fear can open the door in our life to let in a spirit of control and self-

---

7 Joel 2:25

8 Proverbs 3:7, as well as many other verses

9 Proverbs 9:10

protection which results in so much damage. So what will it be? Will you allow your life to be ruled by the illusion of fear? Will you allow your life to be restricted to only a small percentage of what God has planned for you?

What if you dared to stand up to the enemy of fear and looked past him into the face of your wonderful Savior Who rides a white horse and longs to protect you? What if you looked past fear into the fullness of the reality of heaven? What if in the power of that reality, you resisted and cast out the enemy of fear and chose to live instead in the reality of the eternal Abba Father in Whose presence there is not fear?

Fear and faith simply cannot co-exist. Which will you choose?

"*Confidence...*
thrives on honesty, on honor...
on faithful protection and
UNSELFISH PERFORMANCE.
Without them it cannot live."

Franklin D. Roosevelt

CHAPTER EIGHT
Respect and Honor, the Antidote

What is respect? What is honor?

Respect—*Esteem for, or a sense of the worth or excellence of a person*

Honor—*High respect, as for worth, merit, or rank (Webster's dictionary)*

Ephesians 5:33b (Amplified) "And let the wife see that she respects *and* reverences her husband [that she notices him, regards him, honors him, prefers him, venerates, and esteems him; and that she defers to him, praises him, and loves and admires him exceedingly]."

I believe with all my heart that respect and honor are the exact opposite of the matriarchal spirit. Respect empowers a woman to reach her full potential as a helpmeet. Respect is the hidden key to energizing and empowering your husband, and honor is the heart attitude that keeps God's heart for your marriage in focus.

The longer I live, the more convinced I am that honor and respect are birthed in the throne room of heaven. The more time I spend in the presence of the Father, seated with Him,[10] listening to Him and enjoying Him, the more natural it is for me to respect and honor. There is something very powerful about sitting in my spirit at the feet of Jesus and having my attitudes, thoughts and actions out on the table for inspection. Whatever fits in that

10 Ephesians 2:6

holy place will work effectively in my life and relationships. In that holy place we are free of earth's twisted mindset and our own selfishness, free to see the true nature of things. It is there we learn to trust because there is nothing to fear there. There is no place for control there either, because His presence dwarfs our finite self. It is there we start over and are made new in Him. How much time do you spend there?

Respect is an attitude of the heart that comes out in loving actions and words

We women are all about loving and being loved unconditionally, but often do not understand very well what it means to respect and honor. Let's read Ephesians 5:33 again carefully."However, let each man of you [without exception] love his wife as [being in a sense] his very own self; and let the wife see that she respects *and* reverences her husband [that she notices him, regards him, honors him, prefers him, venerates, and esteems him; and that she defers to him, praises him, and loves and admires him exceedingly]."

Almost every time I read that verse it strikes me as all-encompassing. It is not only a beautiful picture of what an earthly relationship can be, but it also mirrors the heavenly relationship of Christ with the church. Why, oh why, is it so easy for us to see the one and not the other?

Ephesians 5:22 even uses that poignant phrase "as unto the Lord" when talking about how a wife should treat her husband. Now, I don't know about you, but if the Lord showed up in visible form at my house I would hasten to roll out the red carpet! Seriously, I would make Him as comfortable as I could, I would give Him the best that I had, I would hang onto every word He spoke, and I would cater joyfully to His every whim and wish! I would never think of degrading Him or belittling Him in any way. I would be courteous, kind, and respectful. Are you getting the picture?

Why does our flesh recoil at such a picture applied to our husbands? Seriously, ask yourself the question. What part of you does not want to line up with the picture that God painted of Christ and the church and then applied to our marriage relationship? Could it be that you have been swayed by the earthly, human reasoning around us? Could it possibly be true that you have opened yourself up to the lies of the enemy and believed them? Is there a possibility that you have been under the influence of the matriarchal spirit and are feeling the poisonous arrows it has shot at your soul?

Our society today has bought into many false concepts surrounding this subject. If a man doesn't show his wife unconditional love he is quickly labeled as an unloving jerk. Even if the wife is being cruel and disrespectful, it is considered the man's fault. Should he love her? Absolutely! I just want to know why the other side has been ignored. Where is the unconditional respect you are to offer your husband even when (gasp!) he doesn't deserve it? The very same verse we use to say a man should unconditionally love his wife also says point blank that wives are to reverence, respect, and honor their husbands.

I don't always deserve my husband's love. Sometimes I make wrong choices and behave poorly. I am so grateful for Steve's unconditional love, especially in those times. It reminds me that I too have a responsibility to respect him when he makes a mistake or inadvertently hurts me.

Doesn't it all come back to whether we are living our lives for others or protecting ourselves? Either we are living God's life or living our own willful, "safe" way.

Respect is a gift you give and a choice you make

One of the questions I am frequently asked is, "What if I don't feel respect for my husband?" I usually counter with the question, "What if he doesn't feel love for you?" It's funny how a simple little question can put things into perspective. Do you always feel like doing your work? No, but you do it because it is the right thing to do, and because there will eventually be serious consequences if you don't.

It is not about your husband deserving respect; it is about his needing it. He was created by God to need your respect. Whether or not you give it is your choice. God chose you to be the bearer of that blessing in your husband's life. You can choose to be as generous or as stingy as you wish, but know that your husband will "magically" rise to the level that you respect him. Oh yes, he may do okay on his own, but the world will never see to what height he might have risen under the gentle influence of his wife's respect. We hold so much potential and power in our hands!

Are you treating your husband as you would the Lord? Do your life and your words communicate clearly to him, "I love you, I respect you, I honor you, you are the king of our home and pleasing you means more to me than what anyone else thinks or says"? You will never convince your husband that you truly love him if your life is communicating that you disrespect him.

To a man, the feeling of being loved is spelled R-E-S-P-E-C-T. What are you communicating to your husband? Would he say about you that you cheerfully and carefully follow his wishes and plans, or would he have to say that you have swallowed the world's reasoning and taken your own way, demanding your own rights, wounding him in the process?

Before you burn me at the stake, please read this verse and consider carefully.

1 Peter 3:1 (Amplified) "In like manner, you married women, be submissive to your own husbands [subordinate yourselves as being secondary to and dependent on them, and adapt yourselves to them], so that even if any do not obey the Word [of God], they may be won over not by discussion but by the [godly] lives of their wives."

Okay, in today's world that is a mouthful. To have the dreaded word "submission" and the words "adapt yourself to [him]" all in one sentence is a big stretch for our culture. This begs the question, "Whose voice will we listen to and obey?" Will we listen to our human excuses from the degenerate culture we live in, or will we choose to turn and line up with the One Who wrote the Bible for our good? Yes, I know that will put you at odds with common thought patterns of people around you. Does that matter to you? It shouldn't.

Fasten your eyes on your heavenly Bridegroom and purpose to honor and respect Him by obeying His commands. As you do this, you will find a much greater freedom to respect and honor your husband. Perhaps one of the reasons we find it so hard to obey and respect our husbands is because we have bought into the lie that God's only concern is loving **us**. He once reminded us, "If you love me, keep my commandments." How disrespected He must feel at times!

Let's make the right choice and give the good gift.

Respect is a God-given desire in a man; it makes him feel loved

As I mentioned earlier, to a man the equivalent of love is respect. The secret to motivating your husband is to meet the deepest need of his heart. He is no more a wretched male chauvinist for desiring respect than you are a spoiled and haughty prima donna simply because you desire to be loved.

Ladies, let me share something with you. Somewhere under all those muscles and calluses there is a little boy in your husband. That little boy feeds and grows off of respect and honor. It is his softer side, the nurturing part of him. If you cultivate that in him, it will grow. And what woman doesn't want more tender love and gentle care from her husband?

Think of his life as a garden. If you are continually pointing out and watering and cultivating the weeds, guess what will grow? Yes, the weeds. But what if you would ever so tenderly care for all the flowers in his garden? Even if you are convinced there is only one flower in the entire garden? Just try pouring all your care and attention into that flower and watch what happens. Just watch that flower grow and crowd out the weeds as it produces even more flowers!

Commit yourself to cherish the tender little boy underneath all the tough exterior of your husband, and you will thank yourself (and me) over and over. Because truly, it is that part of a man that will passionately and steadfastly love you when it feels respected and honored. It is that part that, when properly nourished and cared for, will rise up to serve you, defend you and, if necessary, die for you. There is almost no limit to the level of serving, giving, care, and protection from a man whose wife respects and honors him well.

I could tell you many stories of women who have followed this advice, and whose husbands lavished them with extravagant gifts out of the gratitude and love that simple respect produced in their hearts, but I won't. I won't because that is not the point. I don't want you to respect your husband for what you will gain; I want you to respect him because it is the right thing to do.

Evidently we have a lot of work to do, because the last poll I read about this subject claimed that almost 90 percent of men said they felt disrespected. That is the society we live in. Will you make a difference? Will you choose to trust God enough to believe that what He says works, or will you make excuses and demand that your husband love you unconditionally and perfectly before you think about doing your part?

Too often, keeping yourself "safe" trumps even the voice of God. Control is such a slippery snake! I have developed a standard answer to the often-asked question, "Who makes the first move?" when women are regaling me with tales of their inability to respect because of inconsistencies in their husbands. I simply tell them that whoever is more mature in the Lord will move first in obedience to the Lord regardless of what their spouse does! It's funny how that usually changes the tone of the conversation.

Respect looks at your husband through eyes of eternity

The mirror of human life reflects insecurities, flaws, and failures. The matriarchal spirit loves to parade this mirror in front of our face in hopes that we will look at both ourselves and our husbands through this critical glass. It points its finger so we don't miss even the slightest blemish, real or imagined. From there our protective minds go on high alert to shield ourselves from such horrible human capabilities!

Our heavenly Father, on the other hand, will gently lead us away from that looking glass (if we will let Him) and take us to what I call the God mirror. Oh, the view is so different! It's like being able to look into the future and see the potential of "Christ in you the hope of glory." And when you look at your husband through this mirror, you get a glimpse of the possibilities. Instead of all the wrinkles, flaws and blemishes, there is righteousness, power and true authority staring back at you, a knight in shining armor ready to rescue your distressed self. A lover, a true companion, your best friend, your fearless protector—all in one package.

Think of the power of speaking and relating to him entirely through that mirror! Can you even begin to imagine what amazing things could happen to him, to you and to everyone around you? What amazing power, and what a chance to impact the world!

Proverbs 14:1 says, "Every wise woman buildeth her house: but the foolish plucketh it down with her hands." Again, the choice is yours. Will you choose life and wisdom?

Respect can be hard work, but it works

Respect will not always feel easy or natural. It is a spiritual mindset you need to fight for. It goes against the human reasoning that says, "Take care of yourself first," and instead chooses to trust and surrender. Ask God to renew your mind and to help you break the disrespectful habits you have formed. Remember that anything of value is worth fighting for.

If you want to be loved by your husband then you must respect him. But more importantly, you must respect him because that is what God says works best. A man will not have warm feelings of love and tenderness toward a wife who disrespects him.

Sandy sent me a picture of herself on the morning of a date night with her husband. I was shocked when I saw her closely cropped hair since I knew her husband wouldn't approve. I cautiously asked her what her husband thought about the new haircut.

"Oh, he doesn't know!" she told me.

I pressed on, "Is it something he likes and approves of?" She snorted her disgust and replied, "Well if he loves me he will just have to get over it!"

Let me translate that for you. What Sandy was really saying was, "What I want is more important to me than obeying God and honoring my husband. I will take my own willful way regardless of the consequences, and he just needs to love me unconditionally."

How's that for communication?

I've had far too many women tell me scornfully, "He wants me to do so and so (you fill in the blanks) and I can't see any reason why I should." Or, "He wants me to ______ and that is just stupid!" Oh really? Is it stupid just because you don't understand it? Come on! We are more grown up than that, aren't we? Come to think of it, Eve couldn't seem to understand why she shouldn't eat the fruit, and look at what it cost us. Think back to your days of dating when you tried so much to make him happy. Why is that now stupid?

It doesn't have to make sense to you. If he feels respected by it, then do it. If he doesn't, then don't. It is that simple. In fact, it's so simple we often miss it.

I choose to agree with God's way. Why would I be foolish enough to believe that Satan's way is better?

A man is designed by God to protect and provide. Do you know how you can help him do that? When a man feels respected, he will be energized and willing to protect and provide, and much more.

A woman is designed by God to be a wife, a mother and a helper made perfectly suitable to her husband. Those masculine and feminine roles are beautifully complimentary to each other. Marriage is a partnership, but it is not an equal partnership. Both roles are equal in importance, but they are not equal in responsibility. According to Ephesians 5:23 God created me to be my husband's helper. May I dodge the stones long enough to go on record today as being old fashioned enough to believe this! Let's read our verse again: Ephesians 5:33 "Nevertheless let every one of you in particular so love his wife even as himself; and the wife see that she reverence her husband."

According to this verse, my job as a wife is to bolster and energize my husband, focusing on making him more productive and efficient at what he does. That means I am not on the board of directors with veto power. It means I am not the one calling the shots or charting direction. It means I am called to defer to his direction and plans.

I am fully aware that this is not a popular theory today, but I challenge you to put on the mind of Christ. Remember that God's kingdom works differently than the human mind. Just look around at what is being produced from the human approach to "equality." Friends, it's not pretty. Divorce is at an all-time high, and homes are dissolving left and right.

I wish everyone could experience what I have in marriage. I didn't marry a perfect man by any means. In fact, he came with a lot of deep wounds and distrust for women. What I found in respecting and admiring him, though, was a gold mine of love, tenderness and protection. I learned how restful it was to not have to control everything. For the first time in my life, I felt truly safe. Steve completes me and makes me a better whole, and I like to think that I do the same for him. To be so liberated to walk in my God-designed role of second in command in the home has been an amazing and life-giving experience. I highly recommend it!

Just as people get uneasy and uncomfortable when a vice president tries to take control of a company, so a wife's control and disrespect causes a great discomfort and uneasiness in the family. Usually the children bear most of the wounds this spirit causes in the home.

A while ago I had a lady (or maybe I should just say a woman) verbally tear into me. She told me in no uncertain terms that what I believe and teach about this is degrading, crushes women and gives all the power to the men. She railed for some time, and I listened, all the while clearly hearing the pain of her wounds. Finally I asked her if she could honestly tell me that she and her like-minded friends are as happy and satisfied in their marriages as I am in mine. She hung her head and had nothing left to say.

How often do we unknowingly try to twist the Word of God to accommodate the wounds of our heart? How often do we allow past wounding experiences to have precedence over what our heavenly Father says? I often hear, "I know that's what the Bible says, but surely it can't mean that." Women tell me why from their experience that scripture just can't fit.

Friends, this spirit of control is NOT your friend! It whispers of "safety" and "reason" but it truly desires to destroy your life and your marriage, to steal the joy right out of your existence. It pokes and stabs you in hopes you will blame the pain it causes you on your husband or on God. It argues so convincingly that God's ways are outdated and inapplicable for today. It wants to kill you, and you must treat it as the deadly enemy it is!

Respect is admiration in action

My friend, you need to be intentional about going out of your way to make sure your husband feels, hears, and sees how much you admire and love him. You may think you married an impervious hunk of a man who is all muscle and confidence, but don't forget that under all those muscles and toughness is the little boy who needs the nourishment of admiration and respect in order to grow.

Tell him verbally and with your actions that:

- You believe in him
- You respect him as a man and leader
- You will cheerfully walk beside him and aid him on his journey
- You are a safe place for him
- No matter what, you always have his best in mind

If you can accomplish those things you will be well on your way to the wonderful intimate marriage of your dreams.

Did you know that men have a deep inner longing to verbally hear our admiration of their abilities, ideas, dreams and even their looks and manly qualities?

Admiration is one of the keys to winning and keeping a man's love and devotion. I cannot overemphasize this point. You can give admiration and respect, or you can give nagging and criticism. Which would you want to come home to? Which is life and which is death? Which will you give?

Actively look for things to admire in his life. Spend time thinking about him; you're bound to come up with something positive eventually. Watch closely for evidence of his strengths, whether mental or physical. He is good at something, and he needs to be recognized for what he does well. Listen to him and engage him in conversation that interests him. You are bound to be reminded of at least one reason you married him!

Then TELL him what it is you admire about him. Sometimes we find it hard to express ourselves; we feel silly when we first start trying to meet these needs. Your first few attempts may be a bit awkward, but I beg you to make yourself vulnerable enough to try, and then just watch the response. At first he may wonder if he is dreaming, but as you continue giving him his daily "medicine" he will respond.

Compliment him on how hard he works for the family. Thank him for providing for you. Thank him for being a leader, even when he says no to something you wanted. Tell him how handsome he is, and admire his manly traits, especially his muscles! I had to chuckle last week when my middle-aged husband came home from the gym and made sure I felt his newly strengthened muscles.

There are many differences between women and men that I could touch on, but there is one in particular that deserves mention. I believe it is very important for us to understand that every man has something I call his sensitive ego. Inside every man, no matter how tough and macho, no matter how business savvy or how financially successful, tall or short, fat or skinny, young or old, is hidden an ego or what we have been referring to as a little boy.

You've probably heard it said that a man is just a boy with bigger toys. Because egos are more of a masculine thing, it is easy for us women to ignore them, or worse yet, to scorn them. Our feminist society openly ridicules and scorns a male ego. Young women are growing up in today's world with little respect or regard for men's feelings. In fact, in many situations there is no place given at all for a man and how he feels.

Do you want to get in on a very valuable secret? How would you like to tap into the deep well of love and tenderness in your husband? Here is the secret: the more you protect and nurture your husband's ego, the more that you will prime him to nurture, protect and love you. Never, ever belittle your man! Your job is to encourage and support and to fan the flame of who he is. Yes, be honest, but remember, your husband works all day in a dog-eat-dog environment. Please don't be the one to pour water on his dreams or ambitions. My husband isn't perfect, but he doesn't need me to remind him of that.

Think about our hard line women's lib friends. Are they reaping nurture, protection and love in their marriages? I think not. A man cannot stand to have his masculinity belittled, ridiculed or treated with indifference. Lacking insight into this simple truth causes untold misunderstandings between men and women.

This is where Satan loves to use our past against us. Because we know things about our spouse that no one else does, and because we know where his tender spots are, we can reach out in an argument and put our finger right on one of those old wounds. This is extremely damaging to a relationship. He will walk away feeling disrespected and unwilling to open up in the future.

If you want to be his closest friend, then stand by his side, be gentle with his ego and believe in him. Be active and vocal in showing your respect and admiration. You won't be sorry.

To respect him is to accept him

Acceptance is allowing our husbands to be the men they are. We accept their ways, their hopes and their dreams. We accept their interests, their ideas, their strengths and their weaknesses. We accept the little quirks that define their personalities for better or for worse. In doing so, we are accepting their right to be themselves, just as we want to be accepted.

Acceptance doesn't mean you are merely tolerating your husband. Rather, acceptance is a place of happy rest and peace of mind realizing that your responsibility is not to give him a makeover but to appreciate him for who he is.

It is all in what we focus on and cultivate. If we focus on the weeds of his life, they will surely grow. If we focus on his good points, they will flourish extravagantly.

Here are some common things women try to change about men:

- Poor Grammar
- Bad table manners
- Clothing preferences
- Too much/too little/too loud/too quiet talking
- Not enough help at tasks around home
- Not home on time
- Too liberal/too stingy with spending
- Too hard/too soft on kids
- Too religious/not religious enough

Even though we convince ourselves that we are trying to change our husbands for their own good, that is usually not the case. If we are honest, we do it for our benefit, not theirs.

If you want to create problems in your marriage and destroy your husband's love for you or cause your man to rebel in frustration, then try to change him. It doesn't work and it is unscriptural.

Ephesians 5:22 (Amplified) "Wives, be subject (be submissive and adapt yourselves) to your own husbands as [a service] to the Lord."

I Peter 3:1-2 (Amplified) "In like manner, you married women, be submissive to your own husbands [subordinate yourselves as being secondary to and dependent on them, and adapt yourselves to them], so that even if any do not obey the Word [of God], they may be won over not by discussion but by the [godly] lives of their wives, When they observe the pure *and* modest way in which you conduct yourselves, together with your reverence [for your husband; you are to feel for him all that reverence includes: to respect, defer to, revere him—to honor, esteem, appreciate, prize, and, in the human sense, to adore him, that is, to admire, praise, be devoted to, deeply love, and enjoy your husband]."

We are to adapt ourselves to him—not vice versa. It is how we were designed and how we will function best.

Especially in the days before cell phones, there were many times I had been planning all day to do something in the evening only to discover when Steve came home from work that he had other plans. When that happened, I had a choice: I could either adapt graciously or be miserable. Life isn't all about me, after all. Will I choose control and demand my way, or will I surrender to a plan of higher destiny?

Where do we get the idea that it's our job to change our husbands? Do we really think we know better? Last time I checked there was no vacancy in the Trinity. God doesn't need our help. As my husband likes to say, "If you want to change a man, make sure he is in diapers." I believe the matriarchal spirit tries to highlight things, whether real or imagined, that we think should be changed.

Let's be vigilant and on guard against that choice of discontent that seeks to tear apart our marriage. A wife pays a high price for demanding to have things her way. Let's choose to build our house and not tear it down with our own hands.

Respect is grateful, vulnerable, and trusting

Respect brings out such gratefulness in our hearts. When we choose by faith to look in the God-mirror, we cannot help but feel an overflow of His goodness to us. We also begin to notice more and more things in our husbands that we are profoundly grateful for.

Gratefulness produces a happy, peaceful life. Exercising respect will cause us to be grateful where we used to be dissatisfied, vulnerable where we used to be nagging and graciously receptive of the gifts we are given. No wonder Satan tries so hard to make us discontent. No wonder he hates the God-mirror!

Love and fear cannot co-exist. We lose so much if we allow our life to be ruled by control and the fear it brings. Someone once said that to trust is to show the soft underbelly of our soul. That can be so hard to do. Perhaps we have been wounded and misused in the past and have persuaded ourselves that we have no choice but to build a protective wall for our wounded soul. It seems so very logical to a hurting heart.

Unfortunately, when we build a wall to protect one area, it does not stop there. It affects every relationship in our lives, and most especially our relationship with our husbands. It blocks us from the closest, most intimate connection we so desire.

Will you allow the enemy of your soul to continue causing damage to your marriage? Will you allow him to weigh down and restrict you to only a small percentage of what God desires to bless you with? Or will you choose to LIVE by surrendering yourself to Him and His plans for your life?

Respect defies self-righteousness

Honor and respect are at odds with self-righteousness. When we are self-righteous, we will find it very hard to respect and honor. When we are respecting and honoring our husbands, self-righteousness will lose its foothold in our lives.

The self-righteous side of the matriarchal spirit is a very damaging element. It immediately targets the marriage relationship. Along with cutting down the man and making him feel unnecessary and useless, it prevents intimacy. It is very difficult to be intimate with a self-righteous person.

Sometimes it is harder for us to see our own self-righteousness than for others to see it. It often shows itself in a smug, superior feeling of being smarter and more spiritual than our mates. We may find ourselves musing about how lucky our husbands are to have us rather than vice versa. We may be convinced that OUR spiritual gifting is more important and spiritual than theirs. It may show up in us trying to push our husbands spiritually or physically to live up to our plans and expectations for them. We may even whip out our mental notebooks and go down the list of all the times we were right and they were wrong.

Self-righteousness in a marriage is a truly ugly thing! It cuts at the very core of manhood, and can so bruise and wound the heart of a man that he gives up on life.

I have lost count of how many times I have heard women tell me with absolutely no shame that they are smarter and more spiritual than their husbands, and that they feel it is their God-given duty to whip them into shape. They watch closely so they can get a more critical view of what exactly they are finding fault with. Is it any wonder that I grieve? Is it any wonder that I cry? My heart bleeds over the damage. Ladies, this MUST stop! I wish before God that we would fall on our faces and align ourselves with the beautiful picture of the bride of Christ! I simply cannot imagine her casting disgusted glances at her Bridegroom or telling Him she is wiser and knows more than He does.

No, what I do see is her falling at His feet and casting down her crown. I see her eyes filled with love and adoration. I see the glow of respect and honor written on her face. Her whole attitude is grateful humility and gladness that He would choose her.

Oh Abba Father, restore to us the beauty and righteousness of this picture! Help us to choose Your way and give us the courage and strength to live it out in everyday life. May Your kingdom come on earth as it is in heaven.

Respect flows out of agape love

There are actually three different Greek words in the New Testament that are translated as "love" in English, but their meanings differ in the original language.

- **Eros** – Selfish, self-centered and conditional
- **Fileo** – Simple friendship love or affection
- **Agape** – Unconditional commitment to the wellbeing of the other person. God's love for mankind is an example of agape love

I could dissect and expound on this, but I think the definitions pretty much speak for themselves. If our husbands love us with agape love, we will feel loved, protected and cared for. If we love our husbands with agape love, they will feel respected, honored and admired. If we "love" with eros, then both of us will feel dissatisfied and unfulfilled. Eros brings on the games of out-manipulating the other person to fill our own wants and desires. Eros brings a striving and unrest into our marriage.

It all comes back to whether we will live for ourselves or others, God's life or our own will. Eros screams, "But it's not FAIR!" or "He doesn't love me so I don't have to love him!" Agape says "I will love even through pain and hurt, because Christ first loved me."

Eros runs from all pain and makes excuse for sin because of pain. Agape embraces the cross and the death to self that it brings. Agape love believes in the resurrection of new life in Christ. In agape we set aside how we feel, and willingly die to life being about us.

I Corinthians 13:4 (Amplified) "Love endures long and is patient and kind; 5. Love never is envious nor boils over with jealousy, it is not boastful or vainglorious, does not display itself haughtily. It is not conceited (arrogant and inflated with pride); it is not rude (unmannerly) and does not act unbecomingly. Love does not insist on its own rights or its own way, for it is not self-seeking; it is not touchy or fretful or resentful; it takes no account of the evil done to it (it pays no attention to a suffered wrong).

7. Love bears up under anything and anything that comes, it is ever ready to believe the best of every person, its hopes are fadeless under all circumstances, and it endures everything (without weakening). 8. Love never fails."

The matriarchal spirit is purely eros love. The aggressive side of control is eros seeking to control and make things go MY way. The passive side of control is also eros seeking to avoid pain, confrontation and anything that threatens to shake up its world of peace and happiness. And of course the third side, immorality, is solidly in the eros camp, seeking its own gratifying pleasures outside the plan of God.

Therefore the antidote to the matriarchal spirit is biblical, agape love. Take time to read 1 Corinthians 13. Meditate on it. Read it in several different versions. Ask God to fill you with agape love and begin to extend to your husband the aphrodisiac of agape love. Truly it is intoxicating!

Exercising agape love means going out of our way to recognize and meet our husbands' needs. On a battlefield, the fighting soldier may not take time to be aware of what he needs and may not even realize he is exhausted. What a difference a cup of water and a few bites of food will make! That bit of food and water will revive him and give him new strength to continue the battle. That is what a wife is called and equipped to provide for her husband.

One of the needs your husband has is for physical intimacy. You need to be generous and intentional in meeting this need. When Steve and I were first married, romancing my husband was my complete focus. I loved to plan fun and exciting dates as well as spontaneous times of celebration.

Sometime between then and now, I have become much less focused on romance and intimacy. The children came along, and sadly, at times I allowed my attention to wander. It is important for us ladies to understand that just as surely as we need our emotional tanks filled, our husbands need physical release and fulfillment. Our needs are different. Not wrong, just different. Because we don't always "need" sex as much as our husbands, we can tend to despise them. We would be wise to remember that God is the One Who created us differently for very good reasons. Don't you think that instead of looking at the responsibility of keeping our husbands sexually fulfilled as drudgery, we should be cheerfully intentional about it?

Agape believes the best and does not rush to wrong conclusions. Agape gives the benefit of the doubt in trying situations. Agape does not insist on its own way. It is not focused on self. Agape forgives and is not touchy or resentful. It does not keep a record of wrongs. Agape never fails.

On several occasions, Steve and I have run across people who literally carried around a little book in which to write down their offences. One even had a filing system dedicated to keeping track of wrongs. I can assure you that none of those people were happy, nor were their relationships going well.

Agape is the gateway to grace. When we vulnerably trust and open our hearts to a life of relationships, we will experience the grace of God on a whole new level. When we self-protect, we slam the door shut on the grace of God. We are left with the rags of our own self-defense and an unfulfilled hole in our heart.

Do you believe God when He says that agape never fails? Or do you go immediately to the Rolodex of your mind to scan the experiences of your life and see if it is indeed true? Since when do we allow our human view to trump what Abba Father says? Do we really believe our limited earthly perspective is more accurate than God's heavenly view of any given issue? Do not allow your husband's mistakes to be the trophies that make yourself look good.

When I was a young girl, my mother often had a quilt in a big frame in our living room. Imagine the fun I had playing under that tent. I remember lying on the floor looking up at my mother's needle as it went in and out of the quilt. From underneath, I could see partial patterns and knotted ends of threads. I would try to picture what it actually looked like from the top. I assure you that the view from above was beautiful and amazingly complete. There were no incomplete patterns, no knotted ends, and everything made beautiful and perfect sense.

That is a small example of the difference a change in perspective can make. If I needed to trust that my mother could see things from a different perspective than I did, how much more should we trust our heavenly Father in every circumstance. Only unbelief in our hearts would dare to look up at God and believe we see a bigger, better picture than He does. Our focus on seemingly unfinished patterns and knotted blemishes only reveals our lack of trust and limited perspective.

Ungodly fear is sin. It is an agreement with the enemy, the opposite of trusting God. Agape love casts out fear.

Agape love defies human reasoning. It is a Savior laying down His life for all mankind. It is a mother tenderly caring for a handicapped child. It is turning the other cheek when someone wrongs us. It is a wife loving and respecting her angry husband. Agape is Christ in human flesh. It does the unthinkable, willingly sacrificing and suffering in light of a bigger-than-earth perspective of a heavenly kingdom.

Agape love is not bound to this earth. It dances in the eternals even as it comes to dwell in our tattered flesh. It drapes us with a heavenly robe of warmth and love that makes our rags of self-protection melt in shame and nothingness. It is a heavenly answer to every situation we face, and it ties us with eternal cords to the heavenly world we long for.

Will you accept this heavenly answer and trust the One who gave it?

"Don't you know
THAT WHEN YOU OFFER YOURSELF
to someone (thing) to obey him as slaves,
YOU ARE SLAVES
to whom you *obey?*"
Apostle Paul

CHAPTER NINE
With Whom Will You Agree?

I believe life is not ultimately about the things we do or don't do but rather why we do them and even more with whom we are agreeing when we make decisions. Even Jesus, when Satan tempted Him to turn stones in to bread (which in itself would not have been wrong for Him to do) refused to make any agreements with the enemy.

How often I have unknowingly made agreements with the enemy of my soul even while doing "right" things, making agreements of fear, doubt, worry and unbelief, all while I was carefully doing the right things on the surface.

Now let me hasten to say that in today's world many of us have bought into the lie from the other ditch that says, "I am so free in Jesus that I am not under any obligation to be obedient." That one lie from the enemy has caused so much grief, corruption and pain that sometimes I want to stand on a rooftop and scream! Once again our careful reasoning trumps the eternal wisdom of a loving God Who sees and knows all things from the beginning to the end of time.

Yes, only God is the judge, but that same God in His Word has said that if we love Him we will keep His commandments. When He gave us His Word, as a testament of His nature and character, He had our best interest in mind. I believe with all my heart that He never intended for us to look at His guidelines either as drudgery or as something to carelessly toss out. Ladies, as loving parents we have reasons for the things we ask of our children. Above all, we want the wellbeing and absolute best outcome for our child. It's no different with our heavenly Father. He has reasons. Trust Him.

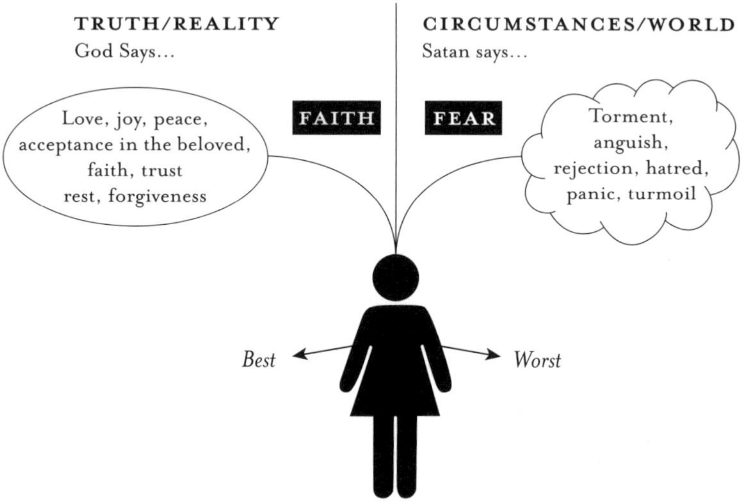

Deuteronomy 30:19 KJV "...I have set before you life and death, blessing and cursing: therefore choose life, that both thou and thy seed may live."

Years ago we encountered a family who was struggling. We met with them over a period of time and soon saw that while the husband definitely had his issues, it was the matriarchal spirit that was really destroying their marriage. I remember longing for the wife's eyes to be opened, but all she could see was her husband's issues, so at his request, that is what we dealt with. We helped him deal with his anger and with the woundedness of his past. We helped him choose to forgive and release those who had abused him, we prayed over him, and they left.

We didn't hear much from them because the wife was still upset at us for suggesting there might be a problem in her life, but every now and then the husband would text and share the new victories in his own life and how God was changing him.

One day we got a call from their pastor, and this is the story he told us. Evidently when the husband came home from work, walked in the door and asked when supper would be ready (so he would know when to do chores) there was an explosion from the wife. She began to rail at him, accusing him of asking when supper would be ready so she would feel guilty for shopping. Ironically, he didn't even know she had been shopping. Somewhere in the middle of the tirade, he felt that old familiar anger begin to rise up. Rather than respond in anger, he simply excused himself and went out to the garage to regain his composure. The wife became even more furious and went into the family room, shut off the TV, and rushed the children up the stairs to one of the bedrooms. While there, she worked herself into such a frenzy of fear that she ended up calling 911 and stating that she was sure her husband was armed and dangerous. There was absolutely no truth to it. By the children's own testimony, their father had never struck or abused them. Oh, but how real her fears felt to her!

In that moment she chose...but what a terrible choice. Since then I have often wondered what would have happened if in that moment the wife had chosen LIFE. What if she had immediately realized that her own guilt made her lash out at her husband over a simple question? What if she had gone into the other room, gathered her children around her, and prayed and repented to God for her own sin? What if she had then blessed her husband and spoken words of life to her children about him? What if her children had seen her run to her husband in repentance, and heard her say with arms wrapped around his neck how sorry she was and how much she loved him? What if? Would those children be living productive, Christ-filled lives today instead of the atheistic, ungodly and immoral lives they are currently living? I don't know, but I wonder.

Choice is such a powerful thing. Whether for good or evil, choices have such far-reaching potential. Every day, in every moment, in every situation, we can literally choose life or death not only for ourselves but also for the future generations. Your descendants will be affected by the choices you are making today. Please choose wisely. "Therefore choose life, that both thou and thy seed may live."[11]

No, future generations can never claim an inability to live well because of your mistakes. We all have to take 100 percent responsibility for our own junk. Nevertheless, we have all had blessings as well as less desirable things handed to us from previous generations.

I notice that we tend to have a very narrow focus in our society. If I have personal freedom to do something, it may never enter my mind that there is a bigger picture to consider. We need to refocus our spiritual lenses to see beyond today, or even go to someone who has a prophetic ability to see cause and effect and respectfully listen to them instead of stoning them. If we did this, we would reap such blessing and wisdom for our children and our children's children!

Is it a coincidence that as the spirit of control expands its influence in our world and in the church that the respect for the prophets of the church spirals downhill? I think not. We love to hear happy prophecy, but what about the rebuke of a prophet or a revelation of cause and effect? Oh the cries and accusations of law and judgment! How quickly the matriarchal spirit begins to go through the prophet's life, pointing out any real or perceived inconsistencies. How the spirit of control tries to dictate to the prophet what he may say and even how he may say it. Too often we tolerate that instead of bowing our hearts and recognizing it for what it is—a manipulating, critical, accusing, holier-than-thou spirit of control. As time goes on, I begin to see how the prophets of old ended up being thrown in pits and stoned. I also see how

11 Deuteronomy 30:19

this same spirit attacks a husband. No wonder many husbands feel as though they are living in a deep dark pit.

So today I challenge you in Christ to make your choice and take your stand. With whom will you agree? Will you agree with God, faith, truth and reality, or will you choose to agree with Satan, fear, lies and circumstances? Will you stay rooted in the here and now, or will you look through the eyes of faith at eternity? Will you wallow in excuses, or will you take an honest look at your own heart? Will you choose to trust, or will you choose to control?

Just imagine with me for a moment; someday when I stand before an almighty God Who looks at me and says, "Dorcas, I gave Steve for you to honor and respect in a way that would make people think of Christ and the church. Did you or did you not do that?" You know, I don't believe Steve will be beside me in that moment. I expect it will be just God and me. I won't be able to point my finger and say, "But God, You just don't understand! Steve wasn't perfect, so I couldn't respect him. Furthermore, he dragged me all over the earth preaching the gospel, and I just couldn't find the time and strength to respect and honor him!"

No, my friend, on that day it will be just my God and me. No excuses. No finger pointing. Just a simple question: "Did you or did you not respect and honor the gift I gave you?"

We have made excuses long enough. We have worn out the finger pointing. It is time for us to behave like women instead of spoiled children!

With whom will you choose to agree?

I do know there are some of you who are in truly difficult situations. My heart bleeds and hurts for you. I see that pain in your eyes, and I just want to put my arms around you and cry with you.

So I say this carefully, yet with courage, because I love you. Please do NOT make an agreement with the enemy because of the pain you are in. Two wrongs have never made a right, and they never will. Just because your husband is in the wrong does not mean you have a pass to do whatever you want until he shapes up. Rather, the Bible speaks about the wife winning her husband over by her God-like character, actions and attitudes.

I am not asking you to take responsibility for his wrongs. You do not need to carry the burden of his wrong, but rather your own. Perhaps you believe him to be 98 percent in the wrong. Well then, step up to the plate and take 100 percent responsibility for that 2 percent where you are wrong.

I believe in you. I believe you truly do desire with all of your heart to honor God and to display His goodness through your life. My heart's prayer for you is that you would have the courage to do the right thing, to choose what will make an eternal positive difference. I pray that you will choose by faith to unfold the arms of self-protection and control, and to open them wide in trust to the Creator, Abba Father. That is my heart's dream and prayer for you and for me as well. May it be so!

I prefer to be a *dreamer*
among the humblest,
WITH VISIONS TO BE REALIZED,
then lord among those
WITHOUT DREAMS AND DESIRES.

Khalil Gibran

CHAPTER TEN
I Have a Dream

I have a dream in my heart, a vision that God birthed in my spirit many years ago. It continues to grow. Sometimes when I take time to reflect on this dream, the picture is almost overwhelmingly beautiful. Its glory touches something so deep inside me that I feel a mix of euphoria and pain. Euphoria because of its otherworldly beauty, and pain because it is not yet a reality in many of our lives.

I am speaking of God's purpose for women in His kingdom and of the glory He is longing to pour out on us. I am convinced that we have only experienced a few sprinkles of the downpour He has prepared. And oh, the beauty of divinity working out in our marriages, our homes, our churches and the kingdom of God!

I have just spent a year of my life working on this book, and I was driven by one purpose—to see the glory of God restored in our lives. I want to be done with the things that stand in the way of His glorious righteousness streaming out of us. I want His kingdom to come here on earth, for His will to be done here as it is in heaven. That is why I am relentlessly driven to expose and destroy the matriarchal spirit. I believe that it is actually Satan's counterfeit to Spirit-filled women of God who walk in His power and authority, doing exploits for God. Satan hates the bride of Christ and wants to destroy every woman as a picture of that bride, so he offers...less. Yes, it's much less. He offers our human strength and a "safe" way to control in exchange for the passionate, unexplainable, uncontrollable ways of God's Holy Spirit. Too often, we take the bait, and heaven weeps.

I long for the day when the picture I see in my heart and the one I see before me on earth are the same. It burns in my spirit and wets my cheeks with tears. It is a burden of the Lord that I travail for. One day, hopefully soon, my eyes will see it come to pass.

What I long to see is the beauty of powerful, vulnerable women of God who are living out their callings and identities in Christ. Women who are strong in spirit, yet gentle and tender. Women who will stand valiantly without giving ground to the enemy, and yet be kind and humble. Women whose keen spiritual eyes spot the enemy from afar. Women who have lived in their homes and churches with such honor that their vision is received and cared for and their local congregation benefits tremendously.

I believe that for years, men "smelled" this spirit of control, and they ended up crushing and degrading women in their efforts to prevent the spirit of control from taking over. Though I grieve at the harsh methods they often used, I applaud their desire to stand up to this evil. By the time the liberation generation grew up, this control had become the new normal, and hardly anyone even detected it anymore.

Men did not realize that in crushing and demeaning women they had also crushed their own strength and vision. As the vision faded, the men began to step back and allow the spirit of control to take over. Today we live in a society that clearly demonstrates that spiritual dynamic. Many of our churches reflect that same sad reality, and I weep because of it. I weep for the broken homes, the emasculated men, the women who are tired of being in charge and for the sons who are growing up unable to step into leadership.

But most of all I weep for the bride of Christ. The picture of a worn out, stumbling, fragmented, masculine woman is NOT what Christ is coming back to receive to Himself.

When will we humble our hearts before God and return to His

plan? When will we stop reacting to the mistakes of others and rushing headlong into the opposite ditch? When will we fall on our faces and beg God to return His glory to the bride? When will we be willing to align ourselves with kingdom principles so that His glory can return to our own lives?

Are we done with excuses yet? Are we done with control and demanding that things be done our way? Are we ready to live our lives for others instead of ourselves? Are we ready to willingly offer ourselves on the cross of Christ to be crucified so that through our death He lives His life in us?

You see, it is the excuses and control and selfishness that make the bride look old and haggard and worn. My friend, you can choose life or death, blessing or cursing. Please choose life, so that you and your children will truly live!

In my mind I see a beautiful young woman robed in white, dancing with her hands lifted high, her feet light and her face radiant. She is being drenched as if Someone were continually pouring out a pitcher over her head. Youth, vitality, strength and beauty emanate from that outpouring. It is breathtakingly beautiful.

The flow of grace is a beautiful component in our lives. While standing in that flow we are washed, cleansed, revitalized, restored, renewed, invigorated and filled with life and peace. Did you know that you were designed to live and move and have your being in that flow?

God permits you to choose. He will not force you to enter that flow, nor will He change the flow to convince us. It is up to us to make the move. In the kingdom economy, it is our duty to line up with Him, not the other way around. He is unchanging, and all we have to do is step into the flow of His grace to truly experience life in a new and complete way.

In that flow there is grace to walk through your difficult situations. In that flow there is agape love to carry you through the painful circumstances you are enduring. In that flow you will find the courage, strength and stamina to do the right thing even when others do wrong.

It is not a magic outpouring in the sense that you will never have any more pain or problems, but this grace is miraculous in its ability to purge even the vilest of sins and sinners. Living in grace allows us to access the attributes of God and to channel those to everyone around us, from our husbands and children to the lost world beyond. Living in grace is divinity come to earth, seen in our human flesh. It is CHRIST in us, and that truly is the hope of glory!

It is the beautiful, vibrant, joyful bride dancing in the flow of her Bridegroom's grace. It is our purpose. It is our place in the kingdom. It is our DESTINY!

My friend, where are you living today? Are you dancing in this flow of grace, or do you live in a dry and barren wilderness? Have you camped just close enough to the borders to experience occasional splatters of grace?

If you find yourself outside that flow of grace, what is keeping you out? What in this world could possibly be worth missing out on that flow? Trust me when I say that there is NOTHING we will ever cling to that can possibly be worth living life outside that flow of grace.

Bring to the foot of the cross whatever it is that keeps you from that grace. Repent of doing things your way. Renounce the rebellion of heart that kept you locked out from doing things God's way. Step across that line and be washed and cleansed and renewed in the supernatural flow of His wonderful and amazing GRACE! Become so saturated that every step you take is sprinkled with overflowing grace. That influence is exactly what our world needs. It is what we are designed to live in. Will you be a woman of grace who fully trusts?

I am only one;

BUT STILL I AM ONE.

I cannot do everything,

but still I can do something;

I will not refuse to do something I can do.

Helen Keller

CHAPTER ELEVEN
What Next?

Perhaps by now your mind is in a whirl trying to process everything you have been reading. Maybe the many details overwhelm you. Sometimes questions can help to bring clarity to our minds, so I have a list of them for you to ask yourself.

1. **Is a spirit of control at work in my life and, if so, how?**
2. **What is it like to be married to me?**
3. **What is it like hearing the words I say?**
4. **What is it like living with my attitudes?**
5. **Would I like if my daughter-in-law treated my son the way I treat his father?**
6. **Am I showing respect and honor to my husband?**
7. **If asked, would my husband say he feels respected?**
8. **If he makes a decision I don't like, what happens? Does he get the silent treatment, scorn, or rolling of my eyes? Do I withhold things like sex or being nice until he capitulates?**
9. **Am I willing to sow into my marriage and cultivate the good in my husband regardless of what it costs me?**

We live in a society that says that if your partner doesn't fulfill his half of the marriage, then you are not obligated to fulfill your half. Personal responsibility is lost in the rush for self-fulfillment, self-realization and self-protection. Somehow we believe that God's laws do not apply to us unless someone else does their part first. We are wrong in believing that. James 4:17 says "Therefore to him [or her] that knoweth to do good, and doeth it not, to him [or her] it is sin." We can never get away from our responsibility to do the right thing no matter what others do. It is between God and us. No excuses. No compromise. How long will you allow someone else's problems and mistakes to keep you from a closer connection and relationship with Abba Father?

Deuteronomy 30:19 KJV "I call heaven and earth to record this day against you, [that] I have set before you life and death, blessing and cursing: therefore choose life, that both thou and thy seed may live."

For your own sake, for God's sake and for your children's sake CHOOSE LIFE!

Abundant life and fulfillment will be found in living for Christ and others and in trusting the details to God.

Determine today by the grace of God to stop going round and round on the hamster wheel without ever getting somewhere. Enough already! Enough of the pride that keeps us from intimacy in our marriage! Enough of demanding our own way at the expense of relationship! Enough with making agreements with the enemy of our soul! Enough with doubt and lack of trust in our Father God! Enough! No more giving ground to the enemy by believing we are better and more spiritual than our husbands. No more cutting them down with our words and actions. No more hateful, hurtful attitudes designed to get our point across. No more excuses. No more control.

Rise up IN CHRIST! Receive God's freedom for your life! Choose whom you will serve—the Father or yourself? Your husband or yourself? Will you LIVE or die, serve or force others to serve you? Which side of the line will you be on? God's or Satan's? Agape or eros? Does your love have conditions or is it unconditional?

If you are already making excuses for yourself because of what someone else did to you or said to you, then you are embracing the chains that bind you. Christ Himself is holding out to you the key to unlock your shackles so that you can walk away FREE! Please do not reject the key He offers you. Many times we do that in hopes that we can control how and when. "My husband needs to do his part," you say. Yes, he should, but he does NOT keep you from freedom. It is a choice; you must receive it.

Are you willing today to agree with God regardless of what other people do or don't do? Whether or not life is fair? Life isn't fair. Sin is a reality affecting life, so of course it's not fair! If you are waiting for freedom until life is fair, you will always be bound. Remember, our freedom in Christ is NEVER dependent on another person. No one can keep you from freedom except yourself.

There never were nine hundred and eighty-five kingdoms. There are only two. By our actions, words, thoughts and desires we are either agreeing with one or the other. Either we are agreeing with God and the nature of Christ or we are agreeing with Satan, the enemy of our soul. It is really that simple.

My heart weeps with longing as I write this. I want so badly for each one of you to find complete freedom and deliverance from every chain of control. I want so much to see you prosper and be blessed in your marriage. I wish so much for your husband and children to be happy and overflowing from the faith, trust, and respect that spill out of your life. I yearn for you to walk in abundant LIFE and in freedom from the enemy. But as much as I yearn for those things, many times more does your heavenly Father yearn and long for you to abandon yourself to Him and find His strength and grace to be enough. He is on your side! Will you give Him control in your life? Will you trust Him? Please don't delay! He is waiting and ready to take your heavy burden if you will allow Him to.

I suggest that perhaps you need to take some time alone to think and pray. With an open and honest heart ask God to open your spiritual eyes to see where you have made agreements with the enemy.

Take a pen and paper with you, and make a list as God brings things to mind. Here are some examples:

1. **Areas of sin and agreements with Satan**
2. **People you have hurt with control**
3. **Open doorways Satan used to get hold of you**

Take each sin and each agreement to the foot of the cross, and repent for them one at a time and separate yourself from them. Ask for the blood of Jesus to cleanse you and wash you clean. Declare with your mouth that you choose by God's grace to agree with Him and to live according to His ways. Tell Satan to flee in Jesus' name and ask God to restore to you the ground that Satan has stolen from your life.

When you have finished going through your list perhaps you would like to pray a prayer similar to this:

Dear Heavenly Father,

Today I come to you humbly recognizing my own sin of control and the iniquity of my generations. I take responsibility for all my sin and I bring it to the foot of the cross. I repent again for all the matriarchal control I have allowed in my life. I cut it off of me from my generations and I separate myself in Jesus' name from all matriarchal control. I take authority in Jesus' name over every controlling spirit in my life and command them to leave. By faith I pull down the stronghold of Jezebel in my life and declare it to be crumbled to the ground. I ask You by Your Holy Spirit to clear away the rubble, to plow up the fallow ground and to begin right now to plant the peaceable fruit of righteousness where control once ruled my life. In Jesus' name, amen.

I want you to know that I am excited for you! I believe that Jesus wants to live His Life through you in such a beautiful way, perhaps like never before. Oh how I rejoice with you!

I strongly encourage you (especially in the next days and weeks) to be very intentional in asking Abba Father to renew your mind and thought patterns and to help you recognize and break old habits of control and manipulation. If you slip up and fall down, then humbly ask for forgiveness and get back up.

If you find yourself in a battle I encourage you to ask your husband to pray with you. Since the spirit of control hates authority, fight back at it with authority! I have heard so many, many testimonies where a woman in the spirit of humility knelt in front of her husband and asked him to pray over her. Many speak to me of the powerful death-blow dealt to the enemy in that moment.

God bless you as you walk out your victory! May the eyes of your understanding be opened to see the true nature of the battle; I am interceding for you and cheering you on! Run your race with patience and perseverance, and most of all, run well!

Frequently Asked Questions

I could have written a book on all the many details of this subject (I guess I sort of did), but over and over I felt the prompting of the Holy Spirit to keep it simple and concise. I have tried my best to be obedient. However, I know that a subject such as this can bring up a lot of questions and I want to share some of the ones I am asked repeatedly. I certainly do not have all the answers, but I will try to bring as much clarity as I can.

Please do remember as you sort through your own questions that it is not so much about the individual do's and don'ts, but it IS about the spirit behind it. God will sort out the details for you if you will be completely honest and open with Him.

Question #1

If my child says he/she can't feel love from anyone, including me, does that mean I have a matriarchal spirit?

Answer:

Quite possibly, but not necessarily. It could mean that your child or you have unhealed wounds that are blocking love and emotion. Seek the Lord in humility of heart and wait for His answer. He does have one for you. Remember to ask Him to search your own heart first. In the meantime, pour concentrated agape love into your child. Remember that love never fails. It is an excellent medicine and has amazing results!

Question #2

I thought I repented of this control, but it keeps coming back! What am I doing wrong?

Answer:

My first question is whether you dealt with it as a stronghold or merely as a bad habit? If you repented of it as a stronghold and cast it down by faith, then I would ask you what new agreements you are making with control and fear. Spiritual strongholds have to do with legal rights. You give legal right to the enemy by agreeing with him and repeating the sin. Perhaps you have changed some areas, but are still making agreements in others. That will be all the legal right the matriarchal spirit needs to have to again set up housekeeping in your life. You need to make a full and complete surrender, and then simply repeat the steps of repenting and renouncing. Ask God to quicken your mind to recognize the enemy sooner the next time he tries to worm his way into your life.

Also remember that you may have habits and thought patterns that have existed for years. Give yourself time and allow the Holy Spirit to renew your mind as you aggressively seek to line those habits and thought patterns up with Christ. It also helps to understand that because our society is so full of this spirit of control, it is all around us all the time. Many times we make agreements with it because it seems like the normal thing to do. I have had women tell me they were trained by their mothers, teachers and coaches how to make better and stronger agreements with this matriarchal spirit.

Whatever you do, don't give up the fight! I know of numerous women who repented of being in control and who later came to the conclusion that the spirit of control didn't exist because it wouldn't go away and nothing changed. It makes me want to cry! I watch sadly as they repent with their mouth but continue their same lifestyle, and then they get angry at God and me. "If it doesn't change the consequences of my sin (even if I continue making the same agreements) then I don't want it," is their attitude.

God never promised us easy, but He did promise us victory in HIM! Don't be a spiritual welfare case. Be willing to do what it takes!

Question #3

If my mom was the one who controlled and hurt me, why do I have to repent?

Answer:

First of all, every single person is responsible before God, no matter what anyone else did to them. Secondly, though you may have been wounded and hurt by your mother, the problem doesn't usually stop with her. How many of those same hurtful things (or maybe different ones) have you done to your own children and husband? What you are required before God to do is first of all choose to forgive and release the one(s) who hurt you.

Choose to forgive them in the same way you want God to forgive you, wholly and completely. Then you need to take responsibility for your own wrong actions and attitudes, and repent of them and renounce them in Jesus' name. Take authority—or better yet, ask your husband to take authority—over any matriarchal strongholds in your life and ask God to break the enemy's chains and set you free!

Question #4

How do I go about changing habits of controlling behavior I've had for years?

Answer:

After you tear down the stronghold, it will take a renewing of your mind. I suggest writing out some scripture verses to remind you to respect and honor. Put them in places where you will see them often. Spend time in God's Word and spend time in the throne room of heaven in prayer. Fill your soul with truth, focus on CHRIST, and live out of His life in you. Of ourselves we are nothing, but through Him we are more than conquerors! Learn to enjoy the ride. Open up your white-knuckled hands and let go of the reins. Invite Abba Father to take over. Ask Him to fill you to overflowing with the power of His Holy Spirit. Commit to Him the reins and the control, and relax in His capable care.

Learn to laugh. Laughter is good medicine and acts like oil on rusty hinges. Allow the weight of the world to fall off your shoulders and allow your soul to laugh and sing. Be that beacon of joy and fun that your family longs to come home to.

Practice honesty by repenting and being honest about your mistakes to your husband and to your children. There is so much power in doing that! Watch even the most rebellious child begin to melt when you repent and ask forgiveness. It is such a beautiful opportunity. Please don't miss it!

Question #5

How does a controlling spirit affect an unmarried woman, and how do I recognize it?

Answer:

As a young girl, it is easy to think that you would NEVER treat your husband the way that you treat your dad. I have sad news for you: the attitude you have toward your dad and the way that you relate to him is setting the stage for your relationship with your husband. That is just the way it works. Oh, you may temporarily treat your husband-to-be with more kindness than your father because of what it will get you, but make no mistake—if there is a spirit of control at work in your life, it will come out sooner or later.

Probably the most common way it manifests in a young girl's life is in rebellion against authority. There is an epidemic today of teenage girls who are CONVINCED that they are right and their dad is wrong. No amount of facts will convince them otherwise. They believe they know better than their parents, and I weep as I watch their lives being wrecked.

Girls complain to me saying, "My dad doesn't want me to wear this, but there is no good reason why not. It's only clothes, after all. Why can't he see my heart?"

Okay, so if it is "only clothes" then why do you not honor him by obeying his wishes? If it applies to him then it applies to you as well. Satan is all about the instant gratification, but the wisdom of God sees into the future. And for the record, He <u>does</u> see your heart. He sees the stubborn, willful determination to do what you want regardless of what anyone else says. You will never convince a man that you love him if you are disrespecting him.

This spirit brings intense amounts of pain with it, as I spoke about in Chapter Two. Often the pain is so intense that a young girl will knowingly make concessions to Satan to get away from that pain. The temporary lessening of the pain only serves to further convince her that she indeed is right and that her parents are wrong. This has absolutely nowhere good to go unless it is recognized and repented of.

Often there will be a rebellious questioning coming out of this spirit. I did not say that questions are wrong! But there is a difference between an honest question spoken with respect and a rebellious echo of, "Yea, hath God said?"

So very much damage and pain could be avoided in future marriages if girls today could grasp the concept of honor and respect! I used to tell my girls that they got to practice for free on their dad. Learning how to become a helpmeet, as the Bible calls it, can take on an art form as young girls learn to relate to, honor and respect their fathers and brothers.

Instead of teaching our daughters to be independent, self-protecting and self-sufficient, perhaps we should be focusing on what God's Word says. We need to reject modern thought about so called women's rights and actually align ourselves with God's design for us to show our daughters by example how to be helpers to the men in our life.

Training as a helpmeet can involve learning to keep house, cooking and cleaning, but I believe it is so much more. Learning financial skills and even business savvy can be ever so beneficial to helping a husband in business someday. Perhaps the music lessons you took will someday complement a husband's ministry. I believe that the most important component in this training ground is learning to live for others instead of focusing on our own wants and desires. To our human minds this sounds backward, but we need to remember that God's kingdom is what I call an upside-down kingdom. In His kingdom, if we choose to pick up our cross we will find LIFE. If we want to be great, we need to be a servant[12] and whoever will be first shall be last.[13] We can live and train our children to live for self, or we can teach them to be Christ-like and live for others. Truly if we choose Christ's way, we and they will find a life full of happiness and meaning and fulfillment. It is not the human way. It is not the way of modern thinking. It is the way of Christ and His followers. A home will thrive, prosper, and be blessed when there is a woman there who is dedicated and committed to building it.

---

12 Matthew 20:26

13 Matthew 20:16

Question #6

Doesn't this teaching hurt women's rights?

Answer:

It depends what you view as women's rights. If you have swallowed the modern take on women's rights to be a focus on MY rights, MY happiness, MY choice and no consequences for my actions, then yes! This teaching is the opposite of that self-centered life. Before you throw your sticks and stones at me, you might want to ask yourself which kingdom promotes self? There are only two kingdoms, remember?

Somehow we have managed to suck up all this anti-God stuff and because of "women's rights" we swallow it, only to find out down the road that it is killing us and the fallout is destroying our children. It is poison! The antivenin is to repent and turn back to God and the order He set up as our Creator. He designed us to function best in the way we were created. Only proud, sinful self (or the matriarchal spirit) would dare to presume WE know better than the One Who made us and knows every hair on our head.

Question #7

Does the battle ever end? Can I live in victory over this curse of control?

Answer:

Absolutely! Jesus Christ made that possible. It may be a struggle for you to regain the ground that Satan had taken from you, but if you fight the good fight of faith, the enemy will be defeated and you will walk free. I have seen it repeatedly, and I never get tired of God's LIFE winning out over the strongest tactics Satan throws at us. God never gives up on us, walking beside us through the darkest valleys of despair.

We too, must never give up. Keep up the fight against the enemy. Keep climbing that mountain. Remember that it gets dark and stormy when you are almost ready to break out of the clouds and onto the sunlit mountaintop. What if you gave up two steps before that? Keep the end in sight and never let go of His hand or give up. Victory is already yours.

Question #8

I am in an abusive situation and control is the only option I can see. What do I do?

Answer:

First let me clearly say that I never accept or normalize abuse. There is no legitimate excuse for abuse; neither is there any godly reason to allow it to continue.

This question of course requires a definition of abuse. What constitutes or defines abuse? I personally hear definitions ranging from, "He won't let me get my nails done every week," all the way to the lady who uses makeup to cover the bruises on her face. In these two extremes, the one who is not suffering real abuse is often making more noise.

There is no way for me to know exactly what is happening in each case or to completely define what constitutes abuse and what does not. Let me say this: if you are in a situation where you fear for the physical safety of you or your children, or if the children are in danger of sexual abuse, get help immediately! Living this way is not healthy for you, your children or your husband. If you are in an abusive situation, you need to get help from outside. Your efforts to control, manipulate, self-protect or cover up will not work, and they do not demonstrate respect in any case.

We talked earlier about how woundedness in the life of a woman can cause her to react negatively in certain situations. This is also true with men. A man wounded early in life by a woman can easily become abusive toward women. Men who were hurt by women often end up hurting women.

This is important to understand, not as an excuse, but for

healing. As a woman, you will never be able to heal a man from wounds made by another woman. God has to do that. God may wish to use your gentle trusting heart to help in that process, but never forget that ultimately it is God's work. If your husband does not respond positively, it is not your job to change him. If his wounds have made him abusive, he needs help from someone other than his wife. This kind of thing can only be truly healed by our Savior. You are not helping to heal him by accepting the abuse; you are actually enabling it.

Call on a pastor or a close friend and explain the situation. Let someone help you see what steps to take next. My heart is aching for you, and I pray for your healing and freedom.

This book was never designed or meant to be used as a club to beat anyone over the head. My prayer is that each of us, no matter what our circumstance, would take an honest look before God at our own heart. Life may never be fair but we can still make right choices in our life. In doing this we open ourself up for God to be able to fill us with His grace and blessing. This, my friend, is far superior to adding more wrong to the whole situation and reaping MORE consequences. Two wrongs will never make a right.

To those of you looking on at situations where you feel sure that things are not as they should be: I beg you with all of my heart to be gracious. There are often many components of any given situation that we do not know about. There is no way for us to always see all of the picture. Therefore we should not rush to judgement but rather fall to our knees and cry out to God to bless them with wisdom and grace to know and do the right thing. So many times we wound and hurt with our ill-timed words those who are already hurting and wounded. I have been guilty of that myself and have cried many repentant tears. I pray that you can learn from my mistakes and that all of us together can determine by God's grace to lift up the fallen and care for the wounded among us. I think that is, after all, what our Saviour would do.